Judy Prescott is a widow—a mother of two adult children and grandmother to six grandsons. Originally from Bristol, she now resides in South Wales.

She enjoys writing and seeing her grandchildren and watching them grow up. Travelling is a favourite pastime of hers, when able to. Not as active now. Judy tries to delight in day-to-day experiences.

Judy Prescott

A Moment in Time: Childhood Memories

AUSTIN MACAULEY PUBLISHERS®

LONDON · CAMBRIDGE · NEW YORK · SHARJAH

A CIP catalogue record for this title is available from the British Library.

ISBN 9781035844661 (Paperback)
ISBN 9781035844678 (ePub e-book)

www.austinmacauley.com

First Published 2024
Austin Macauley Publishers Ltd®
1 Canada Square
Canary Wharf
London
E14 5AA

Chapter One

Melinda stood at the bottom of the 99 steps looking upwards, totally astounded. What a trek! Had she really skipped and ran up them as a child? Thinking absolutely nothing about the number of steps, or indeed the steepness of them, Melinda had delivered newspapers every Sunday morning without fail; in letterboxes of houses from the bottom to the very top. A paper round, she'd realised, not for the faint-hearted.

Melinda was only eleven years of age at the time and hadn't concerned herself with the trivialities of numerous steps, or indeed a massive 99 of them. Her bodily functions had managed anything required on the round, exercise included; that's what it was in essence, keeping fit whilst earning pocket money, so to speak.

Melinda was now a sixty-seven-year-old woman, and the mere thought of attempting the mountain of steps was indeed frightening. Knowing now, with her physical disabilities, that success would not have occurred, not in a million years, the task wasn't even entertained. Her sister used to live in a house on the street at the top; a good job she'd still not resided there now.

The views from the top were spectacular, no question about it. Bristol shown at its best, if the city was ever considered good, or excellent, that was. Melinda no longer resided there and had moved to South Wales over thirty years earlier. Bristol, on the whole, had become bigger and more commercialised over the years, and if she was honest, was now way too big for her. The quieter life now suited her much better. South Wales had ticked all the boxes.

Reliving her childhood, Melinda's memories were all positive, with respect to the surrounding neighbourhood, lifestyle and daily occurrences. Happy times mostly. A quiet, reserved and maybe slightly naive child, she'd muddled through the early years without too much deliberation, or indeed too many negative aspects. Life was normal, as far as she was aware. The families around her all lived the same lives, adults working hard to support their offspring, usually consisting of a large number of children.

Melinda was the eldest of five siblings, schoolfriends having more or less similar amounts of brothers and sisters themselves. Households became lively on an evening when every member of the family was home. Noises, from parents, children and pets; all part of everyday living and all completely normal. She'd never known any different as a child. With just over eight years between Melinda and her youngest sibling, a brother, there was never any room for solitude, silence or space. Seclusion was non-existent in Melinda's household. Peace and quiet! What was that?

Melinda's dad had worked in the barber shop belonging to the three-storey house, located amongst a row of retail outlets. Their living accommodation began at the rear of the barber shop, with a decent-sized living room on the same level, a downstairs kitchen, toilet and bathroom on the lower floor. The first floor held two large bedrooms and a landing storage cupboard; an enclosed garden on the lower floor was more than adequate for the family members and besotted pets. As Melinda and her siblings had grown, in height and years, the front bedroom had been divided into two smaller rooms; separating the two boys from the three girls out of necessity. The landing cupboard had become the entrance to the boys' bedroom, with Melinda's dad securing the division with large pieces of peg board and fitted wardrobes in each room (of a fashion, anyway). Having slept on the lower bed of bunk beds, Melinda's hair would catch on the springs above as she raised herself up to get out of bed in the morning. How much hair had she lost that way?

There hadn't been a lot of money spare, after general bills and everyday living that were, so Melinda's dad had used materials to hand, or low-cost items to suit. Recalling him putting an extractor fan in the bathroom, to eradicate the moisture and prevent black mould in the room, he'd used an old vinyl long playing record and created holes in the vinyl with a screwdriver to create air holes; the record was called Superstition, an old classic and record of the time. Sung by Stevie Wonder and released in 1972, she'd recalled the song, liked it, and had felt disheartened at it being destroyed and used for its new purpose.

Life was all about existing then, Melinda recalled smiling. Luxury, holidays, fancy clothes. Christmas festivities even! What were they? Clothes and other essential items were purchased cheaply from jumble sales, as a rule; a church hall hired out for locals mainly to visit and sift through oceans and oceans of second-hand goods and outgrown clothing, all donated from families around the neighbourhood. Bedclothes, towels, tablecloths and curtains; all dumped in a dishevelled heap on a long table for everyone to pick up, look at, and either keep, deliberate or throw back on the pile.

Melinda had good recollections of buying a tiny mini skirt and dying it a deep purple, a completely different colour from its original drab start in life. The item of clothing had more than paid for itself; she'd worn it and worn it throughout her earlier years and had loved it, despite being second-hand originally. Charity shops today, now taking over yesterday's hectic jumble sale jamboree, but essentially the same thing. Penny pinching where needs must and ever popular in today's world.

Holidays, what were they? For Melinda and her siblings, and a lot of other families living nearby, holidays had represented a stay during school holidays with close relatives. Being looked after by their aunty and uncle in the countryside, and giving parents a well-deserved break from parenthood. Happy faces on both adults and children and a chance to catch up with favourite relatives, enjoying the breathtaking countryside in the process; a chance to spoil the little darlings, out of sight of Mum and Dad, too.

In Melinda's case, it had been something she had so looked forward to, for two whole weeks of the summer school break every year. Just Melinda, spending time with a special aunty and uncle, alone and without her siblings. Peacefulness and solitude; being spoilt rotten, well sort of, by them. She'd loved it; the attention from her aunty, the walks in the countryside, and feeling so special. Aunty Hilda had ensured, from the very beginning of the holiday, that Melinda had understood that any misbehaviour during her stay would not be accepted. The little black book on the telephone table was there to write anything negative about her niece (as well as her siblings), and to show her parents when picking her up after the two weeks, if necessary. Melinda had never misbehaved; her name hadn't required a mention there, ever.

Her siblings had spent two weeks also with them, two at a time, but Melinda had been lucky enough to have her aunty and uncle all to herself. Good memories never to forget. Melinda had been born on her aunt's birthday, a special celebration that had created a bond between the two of them. On her death, the little black book was opened and read; it was an address book! She'd fooled them all, all five of them. They'd all believed the story behind the little black book, and all had adhered to being good whilst there, well most of the time!

Holidays abroad, even caravan breaks, were well out of the question as she'd grown up. What you've never had, you don't miss. A saying so accurate, remarkably so. Had Melinda felt deprived as a child? Never had it crossed her mind that she'd lost out as a minor. She'd been content with her lot, for sure. No complaints whatsoever.

If Melinda was honest, her childhood had represented life as it should be today. No jealousy between families in the area, no endless criticisms or backstabbing. The community was then a neighbourhood where almost every individual family lived almost identical lives. Black, white and mixed race, skins of all colours; people and children spoke and treated one another with total respect, families among families who became friends among friends, helping each other out when needs must. A caring community where politeness, honesty and respect became much more important than material things and indeed, money.

How things have changed today and not for the better really, Melinda's thoughts on the matter. People have unknowingly and through no fault of their own, become selfish, thoughtless and obsessed. That item of furniture seen in the shop window, a must-have in today's world, wouldn't change a person's lifestyle dramatically if not purchased. Not having enough money to put food on the table for the family was indeed a completely different scenario altogether. The 1950s, Melinda's decade of birth was centred on necessities, rather than luxuries. Funds would never stretch to such things, ever.

Melinda had recalled her mother unpicking a well-used jumper with worn-out holes in the elbows, originally belonging to the older brother, and re-knitting a new jumper for her youngest brother with the wool, all completed in one evening; she'd remained up all night until the garment was finished. She'd not had the funds to purchase a brand new one for him, and he'd required it for school the following day; a school show or something similar, and Amelia had wanted her son to look presentable for the occasion. Would people of today do the same? Chance would be a fine thing!

Clothes were passed down from older sibling to younger sibling, and one's in between, wherever possible. At one point, Melinda's youngest sister had inherited both hers and her middle sister's Easter outfits (rare items always bought new for the Christian celebrations), along with her own. Not a happy bunny! Trousers and school skirts were well equipped with a large hem, ready to unpick and take down as they'd grown in height. The original line of the hem was evident to see by all but needs must and the children wore the items of clothing without any arguments, or any thoughts of humiliation. Can you imagine their disgruntled words today? No way, Jose! It was good enough for the queen when her children were younger, so equally okay for working families way back in the 1950s.

Melinda had smiled at the recollections of her childhood, way way back. Had she been content with being born in the era, a period of somewhat hardship, yet, in her eyes, a time for children to be children and slowly learn to be an independent person, the hard way? It was a privilege, something Melinda had felt proud of. Life had had its ups and downs along the way, but on the whole, she wouldn't have changed that much about her childhood.

Christmas then, had represented more a time of spending the festivities together, rather than opening present after present, after present. Melinda's parents hadn't afforded lots of expensive gifts, but a stocking filled with a large orange, an apple and handfuls of nuts was excitement in itself, well enough. An individual stocking for each of her siblings and one for Melinda, smiles were apparent. Fruit was a luxury on a daily basis, staple foods being much more important. Woe betide one of her brothers or sisters touch the stocking given to her! One present for each of them, usually something needed; a dressing gown, hair-dryer, slippers. Seldom were toys given as a present, but ever thankful for whatever received on the day were Melinda and her siblings.

Christmas dinner prepared by Amelia, a dessert of Christmas pudding and custard, and chocolates munched whilst sat watching television, a rare occasion. A day filled with togetherness, rather than expensive gifts upon expensive goods. The good old days, definitely. Melinda had had no complaints where her childhood was concerned, well nothing concerning material things, any roads.

With Christmas fast approaching, Melinda had focused on the presents already purchased throughout the year. Carefully hidden away from the grandsons' prying eyes, the items would be wrapped up nearer the time, a tiresome feat. Recollections of the past and thoughts of so much less, as regards material things, Melinda had treasured her Christmas's of childhood gone. They had meant so much more than today's expensive festivities, and at times she'd have willingly reverted to the former celebrations of yesterday. Family was so important in Melinda's eyes, so preferential to everything else in life. Having already lost her husband and her mother, reality had hit home, big time.

Chapter Two

Melinda hadn't been born in the house she'd grown up in. The first two years of her life had begun in two earlier residences. Born in Southmead hospital in Bristol, a month premature, she'd weighed a tiny 3lb 14oz at birth. Her first encounter with life had started in a three-storey terraced house in Angers Road, Totterdown. Totterdown then, had been a hub of life, a thriving neighbourhood filled with a retail area brimming with well-established shops, and houses galore; all complete with large families crammed into small residences.

The property had been converted into flats, apartments sort of, and Melinda's parents had rented one of them. A small one-bedroom living space convenient for everything required to bring up a newborn baby. The rent was reasonable and affordable, just. Amelia, Melinda's mum, had worked a few hours a week, when able to, in one of the local shops in the vicinity.

One of the other residents on the property, a lady called Winnie Glossop, used to look after Melinda to allow Amelia to work. She couldn't remember her, but her mother had described her on occasion, and she had sounded like a lovely lady. The only disadvantage, where the property was concerned, was its location on a steep hill. Pushing a pram up and down it wasn't for the faint-hearted, but Amelia had managed it without too much trouble.

Her dad, after completing his National Service in the forces, was training to become a gentleman's hairdresser, a barber. National Service, after the Second World war, came into force in 1949 and meant that all physically fit males between the ages of seventeen and twenty-one had to serve in one of the armed forces for an eighteen-month period. They then remained on the reserve list for another four years. During this time they were liable to be called up to serve their units, but on no more than three occasions, for twenty days maximum. National Service ended in 1960.

Totterdown was a thriving retail hub, filled with shops selling everything needed back in the day. All individual establishments sold their wares; none of them tried to sell products the other shops were offering. The owners ensured that they were loyal to their neighbours and their shop's trading products. With money tight, honesty always came before trying to make a quick 'buck', loyalty prominent in the area.

A vegetable shop, crammed with everything fresh vegetables had entailed; from the humble potato to the ever-popular carrot, nutritious beetroot and essential onion, red and brown. A variation of seasonal goods to fill a family's appetite, at a reasonable cost to the customer. Soups and stews were always a popular choice in the 1950s, inexpensive and filling; a hot meal served to a large family filled with goodness, with or without meat. Fruit, though sold in the shop, was afforded as a treat rather than a mandatory purchase. In today's world, fruit has become an essential part of a healthy diet, required for its essential vitamins.

A butcher's shop selling anything from the best beef steaks around, to their homemade faggots, readily prepared using the offal (usually pork), from the bits of the animal that are generally discarded. Nowadays, the liver and possibly the heart are used. Faggots still remain a firm favourite for many today, an inexpensive main ingredient to a substantial and hearty mid-week meal. Tripe and onions, the first or second stomach of a cow, were also popular due to their price.

Absolutely disgusting and cooked in milk, it tasted revolting and looked similar.

In the 1950s though, it had represented food on the table and was eaten as a matter of course.

Better than to miss out on a meal completely. There'd been no second choice being offered. Pigs trotters and intestines, nevertheless, had always been a favourite for Melinda and her dad, eaten most Saturday afternoons as a treat; a dollop of English mustard had completed the delicate snack. Today, Melinda would probably refuse a plateful of it, purely by looking at the contents in front of her with horror in her eyes. Who could eat a pig's foot?

Harris and Tozer, a large shop probably equivalent to three regular-sized outlets, was where the ladies of the household purchased anything and everything related to being a housewife and mother, on the creative front, that was; children's clothing, especially girls, would be lovingly made from remnants of fabric remaining from the end of the roll. A bargain in the era, and items brand new as opposed to second-hand for the little darlings to wear.

Fabrics for curtains and all the accessories to create the look required in the day. Curtain wire, hooks and eyes, and cottons of all colours to match the material purchased, colour coordination perfection. Harris and Tozer was a minefield to explore with the help of an ever-eager assistant. Goods all kept neatly in drawers, or on shelves behind the counter; customers had to ask for what they'd required and the assistant was almost always able to oblige.

Knitting wools and patterns, knitting and sewing needles, lace in abundance and colourful buttons galore, all shapes and sizes; all there to lovingly complete a garment. Items made to create a cosy home or clothe their sons and daughters. Melinda, as a teenager, had put half of the cost into a Singer treadle sewing machine, with her mum affording the other half. Spending hours and hours of an evening and at weekend afternoons, she'd made dresses, trousers and tops, and various other items for herself; a few dresses had been created for her mum, too.

When Melinda's daughter had entered the world, years later, clothing had been made for her with remnants purchased from the St Nicholas Market stall in Bristol. Harris and Tozer had sadly, long gone. She'd still needed to count the pennies then, probably even more so than in her childhood. The old treadle sewing machine was no longer around, broken beyond repair; she'd used her mother-in-law's Singer sewing machine instead. Now a prized possession after Peggy's passing, years before her daughter's arrival, the clothes maker is still in existence now; not used much, if she was honest, but an item Melinda would never get rid of, ever.

The dry cleaners had doubled up as a dressmaker, sewing repair and alterations business, as well as cleaning clothes and items unsuitable for the washing machine; steam cleaning being the only way forward. Anything requiring alteration, taking up or taking in, had been painstakingly worked on, for a fee. Dressmakers were employed to adapt items of clothing or home-ware (curtains, tablecloths etc.) to the customer's specific requirements, completed exactly to the letter. A small business in comparison to some of the other outlets around, but nevertheless, a business centred around the lives of yesterday, and indeed still evident today.

Melinda's first recollection of the shop itself hadn't held good memories, as far as one of her brothers was concerned, the older one of the two. A somewhat gullible lad of his time, he'd walked into the shop one afternoon and taken the 'poor' box from the counter (a charity box for customers to place donations in). Within a few hours, Melinda's dad had marched him back to the shop, 'poor' box in hand, forcing her brother to apologise before returning the item, in person. Humiliation in itself, but necessary in the circumstances. Families may have been poor, but stealing from others was way out of bounds. Honesty was so important then. Not all children were angels then, or today, it appears.

The book shop was Melinda's favourite retail outlet. She would spend ages, forever it seemed, looking around it. Equivalent to WH Smith today, it was filled with reading material to suit everyone in the neighbourhood. Melinda hadn't earned a lot of money when younger; helping out with the evening meal during weekdays after school had rewarded her with 50p (in old decimal currency) per week. The Sunday paper round proceeds were saved up, along with the 50p, to purchase books and items of stationery that she'd wanted, along with much-needed clothing.

The titles of books acquired eventually were valued and read over and over again. *Heidi*, *Heidi Grows Up*, along with the *What Katy Did* series. *What Katy Did*, *What Katy Did at*

School and *What Katy Did Next*. Other titles to her liking were purchased and kept safely in her collection. They are still in her possession today, over fifty years later. Melinda couldn't part with them.

The smell of the book shop, the dust-free covers of newly printed books and stationery items; all displayed to enable customers to browse to their heart's content. Melinda was definitely a bookworm in her younger days when time would allow her to read in peace. Second-hand books were available elsewhere, but she'd treasured purchasing a hard-backed copy of particular reading material, titles to her liking.

The delicatessen had sold dairy products, cooked ham off the bone and other various cooked meats; milk, cream, and cheeses were the main purchases for the majority of working families. Eggs, with the lion imprinted onto the shell, denoting that the eggs were produced in the UK also sold well. Staple foods of the day to keep hunger at bay, at a reasonable cost to the consumer.

Recalling a gentleman named Bert; his full Christian name could have been Robert, or indeed any male name ending in the letters 'bert', but to all the neighbourhood he was simply, Bert. He'd run the wet fish shop in the row of shops where Melinda's dad had had the barber's shop, and where the family had lived soon after her second birthday. She'd smiled remembering his antics; rubbing the lion trademark from the shell of the eggs and selling them for a few pence more as free-range produce! Something definitely not allowed today, but watching him rubbing off the trademark in front of the large shop window, for everyone to see, was hilarious. The X-rated magazines sold under the counter were supposedly secret, too. Bert has long gone now, a gentleman of an age passed over years ago.

Clothes shops were far and few in the 1950s, but those around were very pricey, well out of the ordinary family's weekly budget, any roads. Rare occasions when clothes had been purchased 'off the peg', amounted to Christmas Day and Easter Day festivities in Melinda's household. Amelia, her mum, would take the children out and buy them an outfit of their choice to wear on special occasions, usually; a treat for the children twice a year.

One Easter, Melinda had picked out a pale pink trouser suit for the occasion, and her mum had paid for it willingly; no comments or discussion regarding the price or the colour unusual for her. Thinking back though, everything about the clothes items had been a disaster. The outfit had limited wearability, due to its style and pale pink colour. Playing outdoors in it was a no-go area, surprisingly. What had she been thinking at the time?

Another purchase, over the years, had been a flared skater dress of The Sound of Music era. Melinda had loved it, as well as the movie and the dress was worn a lot. *The Sound of Music* itself had probably had a visit to the cinema at least six times, during its showing. The skater dress was worn then, quite often. A hint of laughter had evaded Melinda's lips as she recalled the iconic dress of the day. A flattering style, a darker shade of blue, her figure then could do the garment justice. She'd been slim to skinny and could manage to fit into any fashion style, unlike today where lumps and bumps had required careful covering up. Growing old doesn't come gracefully; well, not where Melinda was concerned.

There had been a shoe repair outlet, a cobbler's business, as the employed staff were generally known. Their use of a hammer, an awl and a knife had ensured a professional job and a very steady hand needed, not forgetting completely controlled concentration. Learning the trade had taken years; shoes and footwear that required repairs would always be taken to the small outlet in Totterdown. The shoe stand in the window would display a well-worn piece of footwear, usually a boot, repaired to a very high standard. Ready for a few more years of wear, the fee was well worth the time and money spent, and so much cheaper than purchasing a brand new pair. A cutter, spare leather, and strong thread. Cobblers were a huge part of the era in Melinda's childhood. New heels were usually times when most people would visit the outlet, something done quickly and reasonably priced.

Today, shops of this description have a key cutting and engraving service, in addition to shoe repairs, and business is still as busy as ever. Footwear bought brand new is more affordable these days, and trainers are a fashionable favourite, as popular as sturdy leather footwear, possibly more so where younger family members are concerned. Maybe, the shoe repair requirements have become a little less busy, but it's still there all the same.

Shops, shops, and yet more shops; Melinda was brought up amongst shops galore, from birth until leaving home to get married. Her humble beginnings were centred on people all around, shopping for their large families; and essential commodities rather than window shopping. There was no time for window shopping, not in the 1950s!

Chapter Three

Melinda, as a baby and toddler, had been short on recollections of life then; her mother and other relatives were relied upon to put things into picture form, into perspective. Angers Road was a steep hill with houses on both sides of it. Terraced houses filled to their capacity during the 1950s, with large immediate families and housing elderly parents, in-laws and the like; boarders even, who worked locally. Cars were less prominent in the road and few vehicles were parked outside the residences. Affordability aside, the majority of residents were reliant on their own legs and the local buses to get them from here to there, and back again. Life as it was then.

Being a stone's throw from the shops had been a definite advantage in the day, and Totterdown, in all its glory, was a friendly place to live and grow up in. Melinda had known no different, living in the vicinity throughout her childhood and not too far away from her roots during adulthood. Melinda hadn't 'emigrated' to Wales until well into her thirties.

The road had sadly been demolished several years after Melinda's birth, in her teens to be exact, along with the popular and busy shopping area. Several other roads were also destroyed and all the residents rehoused elsewhere; all to build a new road system with newly built apartments and houses, a futuristic approach in the planning industry.

The proposed layout of the area hadn't ticked all the boxes at the end of the day and was never completed to its full potential. A complete waste, destroying the hub of Totterdown, and knocking down perfectly adequate living accommodation, however old the properties were. People were forced to move out of the area, a community they'd lived in all their lives and hadn't wanted to leave out of choice; all without real purpose in the end. Totterdown had somehow lost its reason for being there, its sparkle, so to speak, and although it still exists on the map today, the light has gone out; or rather, dimmed less brightly since the demolition. Melinda's view on it, anyway.

Shopping after the knock-down had required a much longer walk through Victoria Park and into Bedminster, another busy shopping hub of individual establishments selling their unique products. The small row of shops next to her childhood abode hadn't sold enough of the compulsory items required, and eventually, the few shops remaining were turned into living accommodation, the shop space becoming an extra living area, another room.

Melinda's home, from the age of two onwards, now housed online shopping items; a place to store the goods before posting them to the required addresses. The living accommodation itself still held residents at the rear of the property. Changing times, all for the better the experts say. With a much busier lifestyle today and access to everything needed in one place, namely a supermarket, the ever-popular superstore has unfortunately taken over. For the good or not?

It was indeed a debatable question. A necessity rather than a choice, perhaps!

The YMCA, there for the youths of yesterday; at Melinda's last visit to Totterdown was still there, surprisingly. The church, on the same road, became a teenager's retreat of an evening back then, only mid-week though. It wasn't open on a weekend as church services were held then. The church club had housed a room singly used to play badminton, aiming or throwing the shuttlecock over the large net to the opponent on the other side. A game requiring complete concentration, speed and accuracy, with exercise thrown in free.

On the top floor, there was a table tennis table, where tournaments amongst one another were played purely for fun. Ping pong balls flying around the lounge area had become normal, with nearly everyone there trying their hand at the popular game at some point during the evening. Comfy sofas and chairs, a 'tuck' shop to gorge on sweets and crisps to your heart's content, along with fizzy lemonade and tea and coffee available to purchase.

A chance to meet up with other teenagers of the era, become friends, and converse with them about anything and everything; Melinda had enjoyed going there after the school day, usually once a week. Just reading a paperback novel quietly in the corner, was heaven in itself. With four younger siblings and her parents back home, the chances of doing so there were remote and extremely rare. When her brothers and sisters were younger, busy little bees they were, with voices echoing throughout the house continuously.

The local bank, now a place missing from the High Street, with a few exceptions across the UK, was now a coffee shop, a 'posh' one at that. Totterdown was never a 'posh' community, not whilst she'd lived there; home to the working class or poorer people then. The elite members of society were far and few between around the neighbourhood. Somehow, Totterdown had suddenly turned quite snobbish! Melinda had visited the cafe on several occasions over the later years, with her sister and niece, and her late husband; the food was always delicious, as were the fancy coffees, all with a higher-than-expected cost to the purse.

The older buildings still remained since the so-called redevelopment, still there and used for some purpose or other. Local shopping though, all long gone, so sad. Coffee shops and public houses in abundance, hairdressers and florists, all things requiring a base for customers of the area. Gone were the crowds of residences walking the High Street, waving to neighbours and stopping for a mere five minutes' worth of conversation before moving on to the next shop requiring a visit.

Time today has become too important to dawdle, too many things to do with their busy life. Holy Nativity Church, one of several other churches around Totterdown, was where Melinda had attended Brownies, in her primary school years. Dressed up in the uniform associated with the established group, a brown dress, dark belt and yellow tie; the added beret had completed the outfit. The motto behind the Brownies organisation was 'Lend a Hand'. The English Brownie law is: A Brownie guide thinks of others before herself and does a good turn every day. Whether Melinda had, whilst enrolled there, she'd not remembered. It had probably been unlikely, kids will be kids!

Melinda had moved on to the older version of the Brownie, too. The Girl Guides motto was 'Be prepared'. A practical reminder of the educational purposes of Girl Guiding and Girl Scouting. Both were there to involve children and teenagers in learning skills, playing games and meeting friends. It was about trying adventurous activities and going along to special events, day trips, sleepovers, camps and holidays.

Whether the church still incorporates the organisations, Melinda had no clue, but the church with its large bell evident to all walking up the main road, is still there in all its glory. A fabulous building, one that was built to last. She often attended church on a Sunday morning there, after the one opposite her childhood home on St Lukes Road was taken down and demolished.

The regular jumble sale had been held there often, amassing most of the neighbourhood's ladies throughout the day, there to clothe and furnish their children, themselves and their homes with second-hand goods, all in a decent and re-useable condition. The charity shops of today represented the bric-a-brac and clothing in a much tidier and uniformed order, but it is the same thing, in retrospect, all said and done. Bargains were there to be had then and still are today.

Melinda always loved a bargain!

The lower floor of Holy Nativity church is now used as a creche, there to care for pre-school children and their siblings after the school day has ended; until the parents finish their working day. With most parents being forced to work in employment to make ends meet in this day and age, it is a crucial and necessary establishment. A fee-paying concern, not a cheap one either; the little darlings learn to play, mix with others and share toys. All good in the context of things, all in preparation for life in the future for the babies of today.

From experience, Melinda's grandsons had all excelled in attending their local creche, in readiness for the 'big' school later on. The tears no longer fell on starting mainstream education, now an enthralling adventure to begin. Apprehensive mothers could now walk away with their heads held high, probably with a few tears in their eyes instead. Their babies were growing up way too quickly.

Totterdown's main road led down to the larger main road, the Bath Road; the Three Lamps as it was called, forked to the Bath Road one way and to the Wells Road (Totterdown's High Street) the other way. Angers Road and the other roads that were demolished, either started or ended on Bath Road; dependant on which end of the road you were resident in. People of all ages used their feet to get to where they wanted to go, as a rule; up and down, down and up, the steep roads were managed without too many hindrances. They'd not complained either, a normality in the day.

Arnos Vale cemetery was the main place to bury and say goodbye to your loved ones; a place to visit their resting place and remember them, with smiles on their faces and an ever-aching heart. Flowers and small permanent objects; angels, poems on porcelain plaques etc., all lovingly placed on named memorial stones. A constant reminder of a family's loss somewhere along the line, whether recent or a long time ago. With access to the cemetery via Totterdown and the Bath Road, a larger than average establishment with a large expanse of ground it was then, and nothing has changed on that score since.

Melinda's memories of the place include, amongst others, a lunchtime retreat to eat homemade sandwiches and drink a bottle of water on the lawned grass, just inside the cemetery gates. She'd been working in the paint factory as an office junior at the time. The hour's lunch-break was used and spent there, in the Arnos Vale grounds. Melinda's thoughts today amounted to a quizzical 'how bizarre' but back then, to a teenage Melinda, it was a normal everyday occurrence that hadn't offended anyone or caused any concerns. Today, to her, it appeared slightly macabre; a little spooky even, if she'd thought too seriously about it.

Her brother and his school friend had spent a day drinking alcohol amongst the gravestones there when they should have both been attending mainstream school. Two worst for wear teenagers were taken to hospital and checked over, before being returned to their parents' homes by police officers. Melinda's parents, and her brother's friend's parents, had been completely unaware of the boys' antics on the day in question. The dangers of drinking alcohol at a tender young age, along with becoming unconscious amongst the gravestones, where the eerie silence belonged to the dead alone, was horrific when things had really sunk in. At thirteen years of age at the time, the boys had feared nothing; it had become an adventure in their heads, one that had backfired disastrously.

Today, the grounds hold a cafe and an occasional room where celebrations are held for families to enjoy the moment. Birthdays, wedding receptions and similar, buildings are now used to their full potential in today's sometimes harsh world. Celebrations were celebrations at the end of the day, the venue less important than having the guests there to join in. A given reason to be happy wherever they were, locality-wise.

Arnos Vale has created a profitable business alongside the usual and regular funeral services a cemetery is renowned for, with the added cafe there for regular customers to partake in a hot or cold refreshment and catch up with friends and family members on a regular basis. Morbid, solemn, and somewhat unusual; yes, initially, and it does appear out of character at first. The eatery is nowadays happily accepted by those who use the facilities today.

St Mary Redcliffe Church, in St Mary Redcliffe rather than Totterdown itself, had held obscure memories for Melinda, she'd recalled. Again, a place she had spent sitting on the lawned area outside during her lunch-break in yet another employment. Enjoying the summer sunshine with her workmates whilst eating the shop-packed sandwiches, potato crisps and pop (a fizzy drink in a bottle) early in the afternoon, half-way through a full day's work. The headstones behind them were ignored, not taken notice of at all. Inside the large and very popular church, it was a different story.

St Mary Redcliffe Church is an important place on the map and a landmark of Bristol, where tourists and people of all ages delight in visiting. It offers religious services, weddings and christenings and also allows those interested to view its interior in detail, at their own pace, as well as the exterior grounds around it. An old building with plenty of historical interest.

Melinda's experience on that score had caused shivers down her spine and throughout her whole body then; she had suddenly realised that in certain areas of the church, she was actually walking on people's graves. The layer of thick concrete on some floor areas had held the bodies of the deceased underneath, and Melinda had been walking across them.

Completely unavoidable, the walkways to the seating areas had engraved writings of the deceased person buried beneath, the concrete itself. Melinda's thought process had gone into overdrive back then, and she'd not returned inside afterwards, or since, for that matter. The phrase—*someone has just walked over my grave*—comes to mind.

How differently she had perceived things in her earlier days, as a youngster and as a teenager; she wouldn't ever worry about walking into a similar church today. No collywobbles or shivery feelings now, completely calm and collected. A teenager's mind versus a fully-fledged adult's mind, what a difference! A life lived and learnt, where views change all the time, usually for the better!

Opposite the church, a peaceful park still exists, one with a very interesting past, and an interesting history. A medieval cave used to shelter local hermits now holds nearly two hundred-year-old Quaker gravestones. The park and caves, and the stretch of grass, a small area to totally relax in, still contain the bodies of once-thriving Quaker citizenry.

As early as the eighteenth century, the town's 'Society of Friends' population used this area as the final resting place for their deceased. Burials continued through until the 1920s when the cemetery plot began to reach capacity. The land was donated to the city in the 1950s, after which part of it was made into a current roadway and the other part became the park as it is today. Nearly two hundred of the headstones that once covered the area were neatly stacked and placed in the hermit's cave, where they can be seen today through the gated cave opening.

As the name suggests, a lone person would have holed up in the artificial grotto of sandstone, where they would pray for their patron's soul and well-being in exchange for protection and sustenance. John Sparks was the solitary hermit and Thomas Lord Berkeley as his benefactor. It has been suggested that the role of the recluse was a successive one and began to gradually diminish as the Quakers began moving into the area.

Melinda had never sat there during her lunch breaks; the eerie history behind the park had somehow deterred her from doing so. The grass in the churchyard of St Mary Redcliffe was well preferred whilst she had worked in the vicinity. With the sunshine on a summer day, she had been well happy.

Chapter Four

Park Street in Totterdown, yet another steep street; one adorned with colourful terraced houses. It had become Melinda's second home since birth, after Angers Road, that was. Probably the steepest of all streets linking the Bath Road and the Wells Road. Vale Street, close by, was a close second in gradient; a definite sight for sore eyes, Melinda's!

At the time she'd lived there, cars were far and few between, but nowadays the parked vehicles outside the residences had created havoc at certain times throughout the day; all of the vehicles had required a good handbrake, for certain! The steps leading up to the front doors of some of the houses had created issues for the disabled, and mobility-impaired people of the community; that was indeed after they had struggled to walk up the hill with shopping essentials, along with pushing prams, pushchairs and wheelchairs up the virtually 1:1 hill gradient, in places. Living accommodation was definitely not for the faint-hearted.

Small, postage-sized gardens had adorned the back of the properties, backing onto the back gardens of terraced houses on the next road. Terraced properties seemingly crammed into the area, but all adequately proportioned for residential living. Dark and drab really, but all pretty normal for outside garden space in the Totterdown and surrounding areas, no one knew any different. The working-class citizens of the day were more than content with their lot, thankfully.

Residents had painted the fronts of the properties vivid colours, all for valid reasons; to add brightness to a usually gloomy exterior. Blue, pink, yellow, and various shades of green; white, mustard, cream and brown. Creating a colourful illusion of Totterdown and its occupants, the streets around had definitely created an impression, a good one.

Not to be confused with Park Street situated in the centre of Bristol itself, the major shopping street linked the city centre to Clifton. The building of Park Street there had started in 1761 and it was Bristol's earliest example of uniformly stepped hillside terracing. The street runs from College Green up a steep incline northwards to join Park Row near the southern apex at the Clifton Triangle.

Looking up the street there is a dramatic view of the Wills Memorial Building.

Restaurants galore, quirky shops and the historical Bristol Museum were located at the top. Home to the famous Gorilla, Alfred, lovingly stuffed after his death for all to view. A resident of the Bristol Zoo, he'd become a popular attraction and animal celebrity. His fame grew to international proportions during World War 11 and after his death, in 1948, he remained an important mascot for the city of Bristol. His personality amongst younger visitors had quickly become one of the Zoo's main attractions.

The 'mummies' in the museum had been something Melinda had taken notice of; bodies wrapped in cloth and preserved for hundreds of years. An Egyptian's way of keeping their loved one's body safe and free from harm. The

Pyramids and Tombs used there to keep them, surrounded by precious gifts and items there for their afterlife. Melinda had been intrigued by the room in the museum, designated to the history of the Pyramids and Egyptian life, at its best.

Going back to Melinda's childhood home in Totterdown, the popular series, Shoestring, a detective series starring Trevor Eve in the lead role, links Park Street in Totterdown as one of its conquests. A car chase was filmed using the steep street, along with Vale Street; quite a performance. The cameras had rolled out the scene in 1979–1980, and was watched by 20 million viewers on the evening it was aired on the TV.

The last few yards at the bottom of Vale Street, Totterdown, is the steepest gradient of any road-traffic street in Britain. It is unsettling to turn the corner at the bottom and see the surface of the street entirely filling the view forward through the windscreen. Flying gravel, as the vehicles move upwards isn't unusual, par for the course.

Melinda, her baby brother then, and her parents had lived in Park Street for only a short time; probably less than a year, as there were only two years between them both. Being so young, her recollections were virtually non-existent. Word of mouth was all she could rely on and thankfully, meeting up with a cousin and attending his wedding a few years back, had given Melinda a lot more information about her family living in Park Street as a baby and toddler.

Her cousin was pretty much the same age as Melinda, only a year or two between them. He was born to her dad's brother, Cyril, and his wife, Aunty Lil. Her real Christian name was actually Elizabeth; quite a surprise to her and her middle sister, Melanie, years later. No one appeared to use their first Christian names back then, and their birth certificate would show an unknown name for the relative or friend they'd known throughout their lives as something completely different. Melinda's mum was a prime example there. Known as Amelia, her first two Christian names were Patricia Alison!

Melinda's cousin had also invited another cousin from his mother's side to the wedding, and the two of them had spent hours reminiscing Totterdown and its inhabitants from years gone by. Catherine, as she is known, was able to tell Melinda that, as a child, she had resided in Park Street, too. All good memories of the family, Melinda's; her dad had six brothers and six sisters, and four of the brothers, along with her dad himself would invade Catherine's family home regularly, after a night supping beer in the local public houses. There were a lot of them about then, small licensed premises on virtually every street corner.

Cyril had been sweet on Catherine's aunty Lil, who had lived with them at number 96, at the bottom of the street. She was a widow, her husband had passed away at 30 years of age. Catherine's recollection as a child would have her and her siblings, some younger and some older, sat at the top of the stairs listening intently to the voices echoing throughout the downstairs rooms of the house. With more than a few beers drunk throughout the evening, more than a few slurred words would have been heard whilst eavesdropping, for sure.

Cyril had eventually married Lil and they had two sons together. The close-knit family, large as it was, still bonded after the marriage and Melinda could clearly remember visiting them and the boys in the flat they'd lived in after they were married; the bathroom at the top of the flat's stairs, with its etched window complete with coloured glass, still sits clearly in Melinda's mind. A memory from so many years ago, when she was still a small child.

The number of the house where Melinda had resided then, in Park Street, hadn't been recalled by Catherine, and with Amelia no longer around, it was something that she would probably never ever know. She could only hazard a guess but could be completely wrong. Nevertheless, Melinda knew she had lived there at some point in her life, for some time during her younger days. Her next residence was to be one she'd remained in until her marriage, many years later.

51 St Lukes Rd, Totterdown, had doubled up as a family home and Melinda's dad's hairdressing shop, a gentleman's barber. He had completed his apprenticeship and was able to open his own business, a shop near the one he'd been taught in and learnt his trade. With plenty of adult men and male offspring in the neighbourhood, two of the same type of outlet in the vicinity wouldn't harm either business; hair doesn't stop growing, well maybe not until the customers were much older. Balding heads were more evident then, for sure.

The shop, in the front of the property, had equipped itself with plenty of seating areas; a place for bums to sit comfortably on whilst awaiting their turn in the chair. The main chair had an added plank available for the younger children to sit on. Melinda's dad, Thomas, was able to cut their hair more easily and the children glanced at themselves in front of the large mirror, watching their hair being cut; the adults equally checking on their fresh looks after a haircut or a shave. There was a sink available if the customers' hair had required washing beforehand.

Brushes, all various shapes and sizes, combs, large and small; the barber's strap to sharpen the scissors and various other implements needed in the trade had hung on the wall beside the chair. Thomas had also included shaving men's beards and whiskers as part of his service, for a price of course. Clean towels were there to wrap around the shoulders of the occupant requiring his service; limiting the amount of hair on their clothing after the make-over was done! Another satisfied customer, hopefully, and pennies in the till to feed and clothe his ever-growing family. Melinda had, on occasion, brushed up the hairs from the floor to help out.

A crew cut, where the upright hair on the top of the head is cut relatively short, graduated in length from the longest hair that forms a short pomp at the front hairline to the shortest at the back of the crown so that in side profile, the outline of the top hair approaches the horizontal. In English, the crew cut and flat top crew cut had been worn since at least the mid-eighteenth century and is still popular today (with the addition of tram-lines and other designs to the back of the head). The style went by other names in other languages; in French, it translates as 'cut like a brush'; in German, burstenschnitt, and in Russia, a 'hedgehog'.

Clippers, still popular today, became a quick and easy way to remove hair at the back and sides of the head. It was the 1970s and 1980s that would have seen Melinda watching her dad conduct his chosen career at the front of the property that they had resided in, and the crew cut has continued to live on. A cut easily kept, without too much combing on a daily basis.

A regular haircut, or short back and sides, as Melinda had recalled from her childhood days, is a men's and boys' hairstyle that has hair long enough to comb on top, a defined or deconstructed side part, and a short, semi-short, medium, long, or extra-long back and sides. The basin cut, a simple haircut where the front hair is cut with a straight fringe and the rest of the hair is left longer, the same length all around, or else the sides and back are cut to the same short length. Popular back in the day, it had resembled putting a basin on your head and cutting around it!

The curtain hairstyle replicated hanging a pair of curtains in the house. A middle parting denoting the style, with a cut that's longer on the top and shorter at the back and sides. An easy style suiting both straight and curly hair, which is usually worn by the younger generation. Thomas had created simple styles for working-class residents of the community; he'd mastered his trade well and was a popular character in Totterdown.

Melinda had often thought about her grandfather, Harry his name was. A 'gentleman of the road' for years, his choice, Thomas would spend hours removing his long tangled beard, and his moustache, and give him a 'short back and sides', whenever he had paid a long overdue visit. A few weeks of getting to know Granddad Harry all over again, before he'd returned to his home; the park bench and recognisable roads leading to his wife and young daughter's resting place.

The hairstyle cut of Melinda, Melanie, and her three other siblings, another sister and two brothers, were all identical. Boys and girls alike, their gender making no difference at all. Why pay another hairdresser when Dad could cut all of the hair on their heads for free? Looking back, Melinda could laugh at it; boy or girl, they'd all looked similar growing up. A laugh had erupted from her mouth, along with a smile. It had been hilarious really.

Children will be children, and with only eight years and six months between Melinda and her youngest brother, eyes couldn't be on their every move all the time, could they? The barber shop had had a small bolt locking the shop from the living accommodation, but it wasn't invincible to the children, nothing usually is.

Melinda's youngest siblings had ventured into the closed shop, whilst out of sight of the adults, and copied their dad's actions on cutting customer's precious locks. The results, as expected, were horrendous. Chunks of hair cut here and there on both children, both with smiles on their angelic faces, initially. With a somewhat mop of hair remaining, uneven in all places, it had been difficult to create a proper hairstyle from what was actually left on their heads.

The barber in the family had done his utmost best, but Melinda's younger sister hadn't left the house without wearing a balaclava (a form of cloth headgear designed to expose only part of the face) for weeks! With five children to care for, accidents will happen, especially where the gorgeous little beings are concerned. Ask any parent or grandparent.

Today, number 51 St Lukes Rd contains living accommodation and a company called Brave Move in the shop area, Thomas's barber shop, and prior to that it was another online retail business. Brave move provides online fitness training that focuses on the mind as well as the body. A company back in Melinda's childhood that wouldn't have even been thought of, not even in its baby stages. How things had changed!

Chapter Five

The living premises at number 51 St Lukes Rd had consisted of rooms on three floors. The lower level incorporated a decent-sized kitchen, a single toilet area, and a bathroom consisting of a bath and a sink. There was a cellar located next to the kitchen, a dark and drab area that was without a window or any natural light. Various objects and items were stored there, some requiring disposing of, if Melinda had been honest. The main use of the cellar was, in the earlier days, to keep the coal for the coal fire in the living room. The coal man would throw the black coals down the shaft directly from the main road's entrance, avoiding having to carry the sacks down a flight of stairs.

Thomas had, years later, opened up the cellar into the kitchen area and created an extra living space for the family. Melinda had almost flown the nest by then, having married, but regular visits afterwards were spent in the kitchen cum living room on the lower level of the building. It had worked perfectly, saving a lot of leg work!

The garden was a decent size, laid to lawn initially, before being concreted over completely by Thomas, to save mowing the grass, supposedly. The garden had backed onto the backs of gardens in the next street. An outside toilet was still evident, but not used nowadays. Whether it was still fully functional, Melinda hadn't known. Gone were the days when people had to walk outside to use the 'conveniences' or bathe in a tin bath in front of the coal fire. Modernisation at its best, she was unsure that anyone could revert to the earlier days now. Melinda couldn't, that was for certain. Recalling one of her many pets during her childhood, Freddie the tortoise had spent time in the outbuilding whilst hibernating throughout the winter months. One winter Freddie had gone missing and was found several days later, frozen to death. There had been snow laid heavily on the ground that year. Freddie was buried in the garden and another tortoise was never replaced.

The second floor, one in line with the main street of St Lukes Rd, had incorporated the barber shop and the living room, the only one prior to Melinda's dad having converted the cellar into a further living space. Again, a decent size, it had housed the family easily enough, all seven of them; seldom were all of them in the room at the same time, any roads.

A coal fire to begin with, before central heating was installed, had warmed the room up nicely. Vivid memories of the actual room had caused Melinda to smirk; Thomas's taste in decorating hadn't been too clever then. Recalling him painting the ceiling a bright canary yellow colour, along with the door and the skirting boards, had made her cringe. Thomas had then used a bold yellow and green patterned wallpaper around the entire room, finishing off with a dark green carpet and dark green curtains.

Trendy then maybe, but probably not; the colourful 1950s and 1960s had much to be desired. Who would paint a ceiling canary yellow today? Definitely not Melinda! It had also gone through a lilac make-over at some stage if her recollections were accurate. A little less luminous, but more bedroom colours in today's era; a matter of taste though, then and nowadays.

Melinda had recalled having thrown a £5 note, decimal currency then, into the coal fire, along with a newspaper cutting of her late grandfather, Harry, that was sitting on the mantelpiece. Her mum would constantly remind her of her misdemeanour there, in a scolding manner; very stern and austere. £5 was a lot of money then, Melinda's first salary cheque in her first job of employment hadn't been much more than that.

The room had held a lot of memories, mostly good. Squabbles among the siblings, Melinda's room to do her dressmaking in her teens; her youngest brother's war zone with the plastic toy soldiers strewn across the floor. Her youngest siblings would pretend to be enemies, blaming each other for things the other one had done. All par for the course then, children will be children at the end of the day.

She'd recalled Christmas Day's there. Five stockings filled with oranges, an apple, and handfuls of nuts in their shells. A few small stocking fillers completed the boot-shaped holder, for the children's eager hands to explore. Just one present sat alongside each stocking on the sofa. Finances had been tight for Santa Claus and the family. It was the piled-high roast turkey dinner and uniting of the complete family that had been so precious though, memories so endearing. Settled around the coal fire in the room, watching whatever was on the TV at the time, simple but sacred in this day and age.

The top floor had housed two bedrooms, the front one large enough to incorporate five single beds, a wardrobe and a large chest of drawers. The three girls were based at one side of the room, with the two boys at the other end. With all five in bed on an evening, a game of 'who could amass the majority of vehicles passing the window' in either a northwards or southwards position, had kept them all alert, and awake. Through the bedroom curtains, the lights from the vehicles had indicated in which direction they were indeed heading. Points were added to either the boys' or girls' score every time a vehicle had passed by their way.

With every individual sibling owning their own unique space, Melinda's guilty pleasure had been a few posters positioned above her bed. The heart-throbs of the era then were Donny Osmond, David Cassidy, Gilbert O'Sullivan and David Essex. All had pride and place above her head at some point during her childhood. Under her bed, possessions of Melinda's; there to ensure the younger siblings hadn't damaged them. Expensive things, no, not really; but treasured all the same. A simple game of Kerplunk was one such treasure, a game for families to play along with together, but belonging to Melinda it had nestled neatly and safely under her bed.

Had things changed over the years? Absolutely. As the siblings had grown, the room had been divided into two; a room for the boys and another for the girls. With smaller areas due to the division, Melinda had been forced to occupy the bottom of a set of bunk beds. Melanie had 'bagged' the single bed, leaving her no choice in the matter. Her youngest sister had climbed the ladder to the top bunk of an evening. The downside had had her hair becoming caught in the springs above her head as she sat up, after a night's sleep, to begin a new day. Ouch!

As the girls had gotten older, it had been a clothing issue between Melinda and Melanie that caused tempers to flare, at times. As she'd purchased new items of clothing and hung them up in the wardrobe, on her rail, Melanie would, without her knowledge wear the item before Melinda had had a chance to wear it herself. Coats of Melinda's were carefully hidden in a carrier bag to conceal the fact that Melanie had worn it to her workplace. Sisters! Sent there to try us at times during their lifetime, for sure.

If the clothes ordeal hadn't been enough, both siblings had constantly been mistaken for one another, and being the same height and build, it was understandable. On Melinda's first date with her late husband, and on opening the door by Melanie, he'd mistaken Melinda's sister for her. A good start to a new relationship that was to last for forty-five years; Melanie was indeed loved by him as a sister-in-law throughout the years, and became a regular dance partner on family occasions. Melinda's two left feet deemed it necessary on that score, even with an attempted and serious practice on certain dance moves. Hopeless, could only describe the results.

The second bedroom on the top floor had been occupied by Melinda's parents, Thomas and Amelia. A more than decent-sized room, with plenty of space for bedroom furniture. Thomas did have the habit of boxing pieces of furniture in, deeming them unable to be moved from the initial position they had been placed in. Likewise, the boys' bedroom had a single wardrobe boxed into the division constructed to separate the original large room. The items were fixed, never to be removed; Thomas at his best.

Remembering the commotion at a time when the whole family, all except Thomas, had contracted measles now appeared hilarious, comedy at its best. Thomas and Amelia's bed had suddenly been filled with sibling after sibling, after being exposed to the 'spotty' disease. Who had caught measles first? It was, in fact, Amelia herself. As one sibling had recovered, another's body had appeared covered in the measles rash, and they had positioned themselves next to their mother; the second bedroom of the house had become a hub of unwell beings, with areas of their person covered in red itchy spots. Family life as a sometimes normal state of affairs, all in a day's work, so to speak.

The property had received a few alterations over the years, all necessary for the large family to survive and crucial to the progression of time; new commodities were brought in to help with family life and the immediate future. There were downfalls to new inventions though, with the new ways of living; there had to be. Nothing new had come without a cost somewhere along the line. The electricity bill had rocketed with all the newly invented gadgets, all there to make things easier for the maintenance and survival of family life.

Melinda had recalled her dad putting a lock on the landline telephone (mobile phones weren't in existence then), one where you had to actually dial the numbers using your hands; he'd managed to obtain a lock which had prevented using the dialling process of the now antiquated piece of equipment. Who had amassed the latest ginormous telephone bill? No one had actually owned up to it, but incoming calls alone became the norm after that.

Electrical gadgets were sneaked into the house by Melinda (she'd not excluded herself) and her siblings at intervals, only to discover the plugs to the appliances removed whilst they weren't around. Thomas had taken things into his own hands, the electricity bill was high enough, as far as he was concerned, anyway. Melinda had received her first hair-dryer at the age of sixteen, the appliance had obviously used up too much of it, electricity that was. Ironically, Thomas had left the immersion heater on all day and every day, hadn't that wasted energy?

A sneaky smile had erupted from Melinda's mouth remembering a time when she'd wanted a bath out of her regular rota; Thomas had created a timetable, of sorts, for each and every one of them to clean their body throughout the entire week. Sunday was always bath time for the whole family. Melinda, at an age when boys were of interest, and she'd had a date arranged with one of them, had wanted a bath before meeting the boy in question. Had it been her late husband? She'd not quite recalled with exactly who.

Melinda's dad had told her that there was only enough hot water for her mother to bathe, so she'd filled saucepans with cold water and boiled them on the gas hob until there'd been enough hot water to bathe in. Defiance at its best, and obviously not an energy-saving experience! Not usual for Melinda as a rule, she had usually adhered to her dad's words and not crossed the line. There was always an exception to the rule, though.

The old washing machine with the mangle attached, there to press out all the excess water from the washed clothes, was replaced by a newer automatic model; one saving time and effort on the household members. A commodity now compulsory for every family around. With times changing, leaving a morning or afternoon free once a week, or two, for laundry duties, wasn't something that anyone could afford in these modern times. Convenience against cost, Thomas wouldn't have won the battle today.

Penny pinching aside, finances were stretched and any way of reducing costs was taken seriously, very seriously indeed. With five siblings and two adults, Melinda had understood completely. Some of Thomas's ideas of saving on weekly, or daily living could now be laughable, but at the time he'd believed everything he'd said.

With Amelia visiting the bingo establishment most evenings during the week, somehow Melinda had doubted that all was thought out to its true potential, and positively. Melinda, in today's world, loved going to the bingo establishment with her friend and neighbour. Was it an inexpensive habit? No, more like a social night out, and spending a few hours away from the house, costing monies needed elsewhere. Winning something whilst away from home was always a hope, a big one at that; the odds were heavily stacked against coming home with a fortune, though.

Funds were spent that Amelia could barely afford to lose then, and if Melinda was honest, she'd done it herself, got the t-shirt and regretted the occasional nights out, at times. She'd had no one else to answer to, Melinda's excuse, and also the truth. Living alone was a good enough reason to splash the cash, so to speak. Melinda's thoughts and one she was sticking to, illogical reasoning aside.

Melinda's youngest sister's English book in the primary school she'd attended, had proved, without any question of doubt, where Amelia's loyalties had been on most evenings.

Her sister's daily written work for school had entries that were usually almost identical. The words 'Mummy went to bingo last night', were almost poetic, and today absolutely laughable. The cat was well out of the bag!

Finances aside, nobody had starved, and life was lived without too much deliberation. Things could have been worse, so much worse. Families around fared either the same or more poverty-stricken, usually dependent on the size of their families. Melinda, for one, had been grateful for what she had received in her childhood. Amen to that!

Chapter Six

Melinda's first years of living at 51 St Lukes Rd were pretty vague. As a toddler, there were a few photographs of her around the house then, some lost during times gone by, others now copied by Melinda and saved to show future family members and to recoil in pure embarrassment. She had recalled one such photograph of her sat on 'muffin the mule'. a life-size model of the animal. It had been used as a prop for photographers in a popular retail store, notably Debenhams, a shopping experience still around today, just! Melinda had been positioned seated on the mule itself whilst Amelia, her mother, had stood statued completely still, alongside her. A black-and-white photograph shows her wearing a pleated skirt and a warm jumper, the colours of the garments unknown due to the age of the photograph.

Several other families had also paid the photographer for a similar shot of their offspring seated on 'muffin the mule'. Melinda could recall a family of six siblings living nearby, one, her and her siblings had regularly played with throughout their childhood years. Unsure as to whether all six of them were in the photo-shoot, definitely more than three had been there. A more than vivid recollection of past times, one she'd not forgotten. It was something pinpointed and prompted very clearly in her head.

Melinda had the original photograph of her and one of her brothers, the elder of the two; Melinda's fringe had looked distorted, uneven, wonky etc., and her thick brown hair cut in a short back and sides style, Thomas's speciality. Her brother, still a baby; not much more than a year old at the time, was wearing a romper suit with alphabet letters dotted around the lively fabric. Melinda was holding a soft toy, a panda bear, probably the prettiest thing in the picture itself. What were her parents thinking at the time? Embarrassment overload, for sure!

A photograph of Melinda wearing a bright red coat with a huge furry trim around the collar was something she had instilled in her brain vividly, a photograph taken when younger. It had disappeared, lost presumably during house moves. The image was in colour, rather than black and white, a result of the ever-popular Polaroid camera in its heyday.

Melinda had searched through all of her mum's keepsakes whilst caring for her in her later years of life, throughout her ill health. Sadly, the well-remembered photograph had never emerged, along with several others noted in her sometimes forgetful brain. Lost memories of the past never to be re-enacted. It had been a shame and a loss to future family members in the years to come. There was one of her with her aunty Peggy, Amelia's sister, an image of a pretty toddler with her hair tied back in a fancy bow; nestled in her aunt's arms, she couldn't quite believe that it was her. Melinda, well before her barber dad had dabbled with the pretty locks on her head! Had she ever been that sweet? The photo-shoot, in black and white, was missing a quarter of its original size, but the impression of both subjects in question hadn't been tampered with. All good there.

There was a black-and-white photograph of Melinda and her cousin in evidence. Being very short in height then (and now) she'd looked lost and stood next to her childhood relative and friend. Melinda was wearing a past-the-knee trench-type coat and socks that had required pulling up, the elastic stretched, affording them to keep slipping down; what a scruffy urchin she was! Her cousin, however, towered well above her in a short skirt, jumper and long knee-high socks. She had appeared so much older than Melinda, though they were both the same age, mere months between them.

Julie, her name was, became a regular visitor to the family home and Melinda would meet her at the ice rink in the centre of the city, as they'd gotten older. Boys of a certain age were on their minds, as opposed to actually ice skating, and they would meet weekly there for a few hours of ice-skating and boy hunting! Whether a date with a fanciable boy had emerged, was neither here nor there.

A family photograph at Melinda's nan's flat, next door to their home in St Lukes Rd, had her and three of her siblings, along with two cousins, seated on the large sofa bed in the living room. Melinda, her two sisters and the elder of her brothers were all posing tidily whilst a family member had snapped the image with the popular Polaroid camera. All three sisters had worn identical crimplene suits, in different colours, and all four siblings adorned the short back and sides haircut.

Thomas's input into the photograph had appeared amusing, differentiating between the boy and the girls was only evident because of their clothing attire. The girl cousin in question had adorned a long-haired, elegant look, deeming her gender obvious; a photograph to remember for the outfits and hair culture, absolutely horrific.

School photographs, an annual occurrence, had then enhanced the children's profile; no, not really! One such photograph had Melinda standing with her classmates and teachers, all posing with various grimaces in ignorance of the camera. What a rebellious lot they were, bedraggled and unique!

Melinda had been wearing her well-worn lime green dress with a zip up the entire front of it, and adorned a short hairstyle with serious volume, due to her thick unruly hair. Being a slender to skinny child, the photograph portrayed a starving human being with her ribs evident through the tightly fitted clothing. She hadn't been starved at all, but her metabolism hadn't allowed weight to be put on easily, during her younger years. What had happened in her latter ones, who knew! That skinny person then hadn't existed now, for sure.

With photographs today becoming a thing of the past, no longer hoarding up people's houses with film, after film, after film of virtually identical shots; biscuit tins emptied of biscuits, all eaten, and replaced with photograph after photograph of families growing up, sifting through iconic photographs of the day was therapeutic, enlightening, and a reason to recall back and smile. The digital camera has now taken over, enabling only the best photographs to be printed, rather than the whole film used years ago. Embarrassing images remained on the camera, or mobile phone, or were easily deleted; a sign of the times today.

The few older black-and-white photographs in existence of Amelia, Melinda's mum, and Thomas, her dad, became historical and amusing. Saying that Thomas was a handsome man in his youth, his prime, and Amelia was equally a pretty specimen of the female kind. Dirk Bogarde and Cary Grant (real name Archibald Leach, from Bristol itself) would have had a run for their money if Thomas had become an actor. Melinda had sniggered to herself thinking about her dad acting on the big screen, chance would have been a fine thing!

Their wedding photograph, however, had caused her to chuckle. All dressed up in their best finery, Amelia, Thomas, and her aunty Peggy and uncle Bill, had all lost a tooth on the day and all in the same area of their mouth. The smiles all adorned the missing molars perfectly, cheesy or what!

Amelia's downfall had always been her hats. A part of clothing that had never suited her throughout her lifetime. Her mother's choice of headwear for various occasions was indeed laughable and diabolical, with Melinda's own wedding being no exception. The box-type hat and thick-rimmed spectacles had done absolutely nothing for her, looking so serious and schoolmarmish, an image not typical of her character at all.

A well-kept photograph of Amelia with her brother and sister dressed up for the Easter festivities was something that recalled time gone by, in all its glory. The girls were wearing pretty dresses, best shoes with ribbon bows and on their heads, an Easter bonnet tied tidily underneath their chins with a bow. Cute overload, for sure! Was Melinda's mum ever that young? Evidently so, yes.

Aunty Peggy and Uncle Bill had lived next door to Melinda's grandparents, on her dad's side. Amelia and Thomas's relationship had grown due to being next-door neighbours, she'd lived with her sister and brother-in-law. Photographs of Melinda's cousin, Peggy and Bill's child, a boy, were there to see; enveloped in the arms of her nan, next door. Friends and neighbours, people helped one another through life and their daily regimes.

As Amelia and Thomas's children were born, all five of them, evidence of both her aunty Peggy and her Nan (grandmother) being there for the brood was there; proof in a photograph or two, or more. Sadly, Frederick, her grandfather, passed away when Melinda was eight years of age. The loveable and local chimney sweep had died. Her nan had moved into a flat next door to their family home in St Lukes Rd, where she remained for several years. Passing away at ninety-six years of age was heart wrenching for the large family and all who knew her.

Photographs, over the years in St Lukes Rd, had ranged from old black-and-white images to school class photographs of Melinda and her siblings. Never put into an album for safekeeping in years to come, sadly more than a few were lost and others broken beyond repair due to being laid idly around the house. One, or more, had been scribbled on by the siblings, or even Melinda herself.

One such photograph, a black-and-white image of Thomas outside the barber's shop he had worked in, before opening his own shop, that was. It had become a shopping list on the reverse by Melinda's mum. Not having paper to hand, she had scribbled her requirements on the back of it. Luckily, Melanie's daughter had been around at the time, and is now the proud owner of her handsome granddad's photograph; the good-looking man in his twenties, posing for the camera, is indeed Melinda's dad and there for future generations to see.

In Melinda's home today, hanging pride of place in her living room is a professional photograph of her late husband,

Peter; encased in a glass frame, the cheeky toddler sits happily for the camera wearing clothing of time gone by. The smile on his face though, represents happiness and contentment, along with the resemblance in several of his grandsons.

The opposite wall now holds a large sketch of Melinda's soulmate, carefully and delicately worked on from one of his most recent photographs in leaded pencil; creating Peter's profile perfectly. An image framed for years to come for all to see and remember the humble builder, who was Melinda's husband.

How Melinda would love to have found photographs of her elder descendants, going way way back; those she had never really known, but would have loved to have met in their heyday. Great and great-great-grandparents, some with obscure and outdated Christian names and relatively unknown in today's world. She'd definitely not heard of some of them, and would never name one of her children with any of her ancestor's main Christian name. They would have been horrified, for sure.

Their austere looks and dowdy clothing, as of today, that is. Devoid of smiles, the cameras in their day had required the image to be perfect, the first time. They'd only have one chance to create the image perfectly and to capture the moment. Pictures past, but full of history and unique insight into the times of the day. Melinda had loved looking at them and so wanted to see more of her own family members in their decade.

Melinda's granddad, on her mother's side, held emotional recollections of her childhood, unique memories. A 'gentleman of the road' for over thirty years, she'd memorised his photograph in the local newspaper where he'd resided, along with the heading 'Remember Him?' Harry had died on a park bench in the park he'd called home, an area not far away from his beloved wife and youngest daughter's graves; somewhere he had frequently visited throughout his final years.

Recalling his infrequent stays at the family home in St Lukes Rd, her dad's spare clothes on and a now freshly faced and beard-free granddad, Harry's dishevelled looks of earlier still held that mischievous grin and famous glint in his eyes. The pipe still placed in his mouth, whether lit and filled with tobacco, or not; a few weeks getting to know his grandchildren before returning to the park, and his home for the duration of his life.

Victoria Park, local to St Lukes Rd, was a place where, for those few weeks every two or three years or so, Melinda and her siblings had taken Harry to; a place to sit and ponder, contemplate even, and enjoy one another's company, until he had decided to leave their home and return to his outdoor living.

Melinda's cousin had had a few photographs posing with Harry, him as a child; Melinda had copied them and kept them safe. Tracing the family tree, she'd managed to obtain an original photograph of him in the Gloucester Regiment of the army and stood proudly alongside the soldiers he had served with whilst in India and China, for over six years.

The cheeky grin was evident there and recognised for being an older version of Melinda's brother, the elder of the two. There had been no mistaking Harry, none at all. A treasured possession, along with a recollection of a granddad who couldn't settle after his soulmate's death at just thirty-eight years of age.

'Happy as Larry' may be a phrase known to many, but Harry was happy in his own little world. 'Happy as Harry' could well become a newly formed rendition of the notable phrase, for Melinda anyway. He may have been homeless (by choice), but he had lived the life he'd loved and was grateful his family had allowed him to continue to do so. The smile on his face had said it all, a smile that his grandchildren will never ever forget.

Photographs will always be something required in today's world, whether collected on a digital camera or haphazardly placed in an old biscuit tin somewhere in the house. Memories of people, past, present and future; images would always be required, for sure. Educating children and older human beings, now and in the future, photographic evidence will always be a necessity. People were so important, whether living or indeed dead. Lives were precious and circumstances of living were equally important. History began yesterday, for people of the future to discover tomorrow.

Chapter Seven

St Lukes Rd, Totterdown was a thriving area of Bristol, with the emphasis on was! As a child, Melinda had been lucky enough to have almost everything needed on her doorstep. The few shops in her rank had included a greengrocer, a delicatessen, a fresh fish shop and a wool shop; a shop selling balls of wool, knitting patterns and everything required to create knitted garment for the whole family.

The handyman store was next door to her dad's barber shop, a retail outlet selling everything for the budding D-I-Y enthusiast; from screws, nails and tap washers, to lengths of wood, plasterboard, paint and wallpaper. Tools of the trade, glues, silicones of all colours, and wooden and steel ladders; small, medium, large and step. An Aladdin's cave of goods kept in a smallish shop, one definitely not your B and Q of today. Local customers spending pennies to keep their houses up together, as inexpensively as possible.

As years had passed, it was Thomas and Amelia who had invested into the business, when the proprietors had retired. Melinda's mum had served behind the counter, with the help of a paid assistant, there to cut the lengths of wood to the customers' requirements and aid with the heavier items purchased. Melinda's brain had remembered him, a gentleman named George, and he had created unique coffee tables from the contents of the shop to sell on to others, for a profit.

Melinda's nan had lived in the upstairs flat after her granddad's death. She had loved her nan and would visit her every day as a child, ensuring she was okay. Spending hours in her company watching the small black-and-white television there in the living room, just being there with her was all-important, in Melinda's eyes. Conversation was at a minimum, quiet being the order of the day where the elder relatives were concerned. How things have changed today!

A mother to thirteen children, ten of her own and three stepchildren, Thomas was the youngest member of the family and had taken control after his dad's passing. Visitors to the flat were constant and busy, with sons and daughters checking on their elderly mother, all good. Melinda's numerous recollections of her nan had included her cups of tea made with sterilised milk; a very different stance on breakfast tea made with whole milk, and an acquired taste. Amelia hadn't been keen on the famous beverage made with sterilised milk, but Melinda, to this day, recalled the cuppas and would still drink the occasional refreshment now, sterilised milk-based.

Her nan's lavender bush, located in the back garden of the three-storey building, was her pride and joy. Pruned and watered regularly, the shape and colour of the flowering bush could be seen vividly in Melinda's thoughts as if it were yesterday. The smell, the sweetly fragranced bush, when passing by it was indulgence at its best; heaven to your nose!

Melinda would help her nan put the washing on the long outside line, handing her the pegs as she'd retrieved the clothing from the washing basket, passing the aroma wafting from the lavender bush as they went. Of an age, her nan was, but she'd kept herself busy with household chores for as long as she was able to.

With a few domestic houses breaking up the rank of shops, it had been the newsagents' property that was situated next. Florence, or Flo, as she was known, had sold sweet confectionery, tobacco and cigarettes, newspapers and magazines. Similarly, she had lived at the rear of the shop premises. Being a widow with three children to support, she'd done a pretty good job, from what Melinda could see back then.

It was there that Melinda had done her paper round on a Sunday morning, with Flo marking each newspaper with a number relevant to the house it was to be delivered to. Carefully placed into the strapped bag, big enough to hold the correct amount of newspapers and magazines, Melinda would take over from there. Each and every piece of reading material was put through the correct letterbox, in all winds and weather, only returning to the shop when an empty bag was evident.

Melinda's job had been completed.

Her brother had, at one time, delivered the morning newspapers, before heading off to school, that was. Earning monies to afford luxuries, or items their parents couldn't afford, was a learning curve; educational and preparation for the world of work, well into the future. It hadn't done Melinda or her sibling any harm and if she was honest, she'd enjoyed it at the time. With an age difference now, the probability of the experience being repeated was a definite no. No way, Jose! The premises next to Flo's had changed over the years, from one retail outlet to another, and, off the top of her head

Melinda hadn't recalled the last owners or their wares whilst in her childhood. The exterior was painted a canary yellow and was a corner property, that was as much as her brain could convey realistically; obviously not a shop she had frequented often.

The pavement had turned into a road, Hill Avenue, one of the entrances to Victoria Park, a large popular area for both adults and children alike. Crossing the road, yet another corner retail outlet, the local off-licence was situated. Premises open most evenings for the purchase of alcoholic beverages, flavoured crisps, tobacco and confectionery.

The elderly couple who ran the establishment were popular faces around the neighbourhood and due to the selling of their products were familiar with almost everyone living in the vicinity; they were insightful of their alcoholic preferences and whether they were indeed cigarette or cigar smokers, or abstainers.

Sadly, a leak of carbon monoxide into their living premises at the rear of the property had caused their early and untimely deaths. They hadn't suffered and hadn't woken up from their evening's sleep, so never knew of their demise; a blessing perhaps. The coal fires of the day, are the cause of the catastrophe; central heating being a thing of the future.

The shop hadn't re-opened after their deaths, their grown-up children not wanting to continue in their parent's footsteps, or carry on in their shoes. The memory alone was a more than reasonable excuse to cease trading, for sure. Just thinking about them today, had Melinda's arms producing goosebumps; a lovely couple, bailing out of life way too soon.

The remainder of St Lukes Rd, on Melinda's home's side, after the off-licence, had consisted of terraced houses, all on three floors; back gardens backing onto Victoria Park itself. In between the houses, before the railway bridge, there were two small public houses. Establishments were usually used for the male members of the family, for a quick pint or two before returning to the family unit. A break from work overload and a chance to chill, momentarily, and converse with fellow breadwinners of the era.

Nothing posh or fancy, merely a small room in a building equipped with a few benches and chairs, numerous tables and the compulsory bar, complete with alcoholic drinks in abundance. The landlord, usually the bartender, there to offer an ear to listen and a mouth to converse, about almost anything, everything, or nothing in particular. Relaxation at its best, in a hard-working and sometimes difficult decade.

Melinda had had several friends over the years, ones that had lived in the terrace of houses situated along that part of St Lukes Rd; the side where properties had backed onto the local park, Victoria Park. A family of six siblings had played with Melinda and her siblings, over the years, in the recreational area itself.

After primary school was finished for the day, during the summer months, she would be allowed into the park with her siblings and friends, to play. When the evening meal was ready, Amelia would shout over the wall adjacent to Hill Avenue, and Melinda and her siblings would return home for food. The condition to entering the recreational garden, as it was, had been that they remain in that part of the park; not venturing further afield in the large expanse of grass and its amenities.

Wearing the children out, ready for bedtime and school the following morning, had made absolute sense, and back in

Melinda's early years the worry of leaving the children without adults around to supervise, hadn't been a real issue. The youngest and elder siblings, along with their playmates, had all looked after each other and if any bumps and bruises had arisen, then one of the parents would be alerted to help.

Today's world, full of people with ulterior motives where children are concerned, has caused parents to prohibit them from playing out of sight and away from the home. Precious offspring deserved to be protected from the bad people out there; somehow though, wrapping them up from the demons around them wasn't always a good thing, in hindsight.

Cotton wool is sometimes a little too soft and a few bumps and bruises along the way had prepared the youngsters for the harsher parts of life; a stronger personality, perhaps with more devilment and an ability to cope in more difficult circumstances. Saying that, Melinda was always a naive child, quiet and reserved. Her ability to manage on her own though, in times of trouble or turmoil as a teenager, had always been good; Mummy and Daddy hadn't required to be there all the time.

As Melinda had grown, there were two girls of similar ages living in the terraced houses. Both were only children, having no brothers or sisters, and she would often visit one or the other and spend a few hours in their house enjoying their company. Daphne and Jill were lovely girls and their parents hadn't minded Melinda being there.

Boyfriends had stopped the regular few hours at her friends' houses, Daphne and Jill's, not Melinda's. The girls were slightly older, by a year or two, and the opposite sex was now a favourite pastime, an adventure; that was until Mr

Right had come along for each of them. Her turn would come in time, hopefully.

The second of many entrances to Victoria Park had emerged, as St Lukes Rd continued past the terraced houses and the two small public houses. The railway bridge, now about to be walked under, was there in full view and there hadn't been a train passing at the time. Looking directly opposite the park's entrance, across the road, was the 99 steps that Melinda had frequented on her paper round at eleven years of age and beyond.

Sadly, all the houses that had years ago stood on that side of the road, were no longer there. Demolished by the builders for yet another planning disaster that had gone horribly wrong, they'd unnecessarily been pulled down and the residents rehoused elsewhere. Ironically, it was the houses on the park's side of the road that should have been demolished! Planning processes at their best!

Further down the line, before Melinda had left the family home to marry, would see the terraced houses and the public houses still there, demolished too. By the time Melinda had turned fifteen, or possibly younger than that, all residential premises from Hill Avenue onwards, had fallen to the developers. To this day, nothing structurally has ever replaced the homes of the community in Melinda's decade as a child, more is the pity. Times a changing, for the better or worse? The answer was debatable.

Victoria Park, now in full view for every home remaining overlooking it, was given a clear and visible picture of the popular recreational area; all good in the context of things to come in later years. The people who had resided in the now demolished properties, the residents who had all been happy living in St Lukes Rd for years, were obviously not so full of smiles. They were rehoused in Bristol, but not always near the community they had formed friendships with, short and long term. The local public houses had lost their loyal customers, the men of the family out for a well-deserved pint or two in walking distance of their homes, before being demolished themselves. Needless to say, there were other public houses nearby, one opposite Melinda's home for starters, but the choices of those now existing were far and few between.

A pint or two would have been supped somewhere, in some other public house no doubt; regulars of the now demolished ones had parked their bottoms elsewhere instead. Familiarity had been lost though, friendly faces and polite conversation between all who had visited them frequently. Friendships had been broken through no fault of their own. Sad occasions, for sure.

Chapter Eight

Walking underneath the railway bridge, Melinda recalled the eerie silence and the darkness, especially during the winter months. At times, the short expanse of pavement could be quite frightening, and she would run under the bridge, or walk at a faster pace than she had along the whole of St Lukes Rd itself.

With no light penetrating, it had visualised a tunnel, and although nothing sinister had ever occurred there, the fear was always evident. One recollection though, when walking through the 'tunnel' with her mother, had seen her swung up into an unknown male's arms; stunning her completely and frightening the life out of her, momentarily. The gentleman in question had been her middle sister's school teacher, and he'd mistaken Melinda for her. Melanie had been a well-favoured pupil with the said teacher, but was no longer in his class, moving on to a higher year in education. Hilarious now, but not at the time!

The collywobbles would always set in as Melinda entered that part of the road, for absolutely no reason at all. She'd never been afraid of the dark; though fire and flames were another matter altogether. Her fear of fire had continued for years, well into late adulthood. At sixty-seven years of age now, she could just about light a scented candle! Melinda's son would light the coal fire after returning from primary school after she'd prepared it, all ready for igniting. Sitting in a cold house alone, until the children were home, was par for the course, then.

Passing the 'tunnel', the pavement had continued with an entrance to an industrial company, she'd not recalled exactly what they had done. Large steel gates had led up to a concrete driveway, to the building housing something commercial! Melinda hadn't often seen the gates open, so mentally she had obliterated the building from her mind.

It was a few small shops that had Melinda approaching next. Two such shops had sentimental memories for her, and she could still remember the owners of the premises in question, and see them in person, vividly. The sweet shop, cum grocery shop, cum tobacconist shop was owned by Sid's parents. A middle-aged gentleman who had never married, Sid was, and it was usually him who had served the mountain of schoolchildren frequenting the old-fashioned premises.

A dimly lit shop, as Melinda had recalled, but adequate for all to view the goods required purchasing. Sid and his parents were never going to be millionaires, the average customer spending pennies rather than pounds, in pre-decimal currency; half-pennies, pennies and threepenny pieces of the days spent before and after attending the local primary school, St Lukes Junior School.

Decimalisation had come into effect in February 1971, the 15th to be exact, and a whole new collection of coins was then introduced. With 240 pennies to an old pound then, scholars today would be thrown into turmoil, in a definite quandary, when reckoning up the till at the end of a working day.

Calculators were scarce too, so a brain was required to count the day's proceeds correctly.

When Melinda was allowed to walk to school on her own, usually with some of her siblings, but without one of her parents, a quick visit to Sid's before would usually arise.

"Can you freeze a Mars bar for me, please?" Melinda would shout through the doorway to Sid, and then she would head for the school gates.

It hadn't just been Mars bars that he would put in the freezer, on demand. Milky Ways were popular alternatives, along with Snickers bars and Cadbury's Creme eggs, all requested by the schoolchildren; children he'd gotten used to over the years and knew would pay for the goods ordered after school was finished for the day.

With a rock-hard Mars bar paid for and eaten on the way home, how any of the children had reached adulthood with a full set of teeth, was a miracle in itself. The ten penny mixes of yesterday had some children walking home with a goody bag full of popular sweets of the era; fizzy fish, black jacks and fruit salads to name just a few.

Melinda had hated the sherbet flying saucers, a sweet confectionery still around today, still in existence. It was similar to eating a mouth full of polystyrene, as far as she was concerned, not nice. Shrimps, bananas, white mice and cola bottles, others she'd recalled and had liked; pink pigs, and giant white chocolate buttons sprinkled with hundreds and thousands. Melinda's mouth was watering, for sure.

The summer had called for the extra-long tip tops, in various flavours, and huge jubilee triangular lollies. Ice cold and full of tasty juice, Sid's freezer was crammed to the top in readiness for the children to purchase them and delight in eating on their way home from school. Groups of youngsters were seen walking up St Lukes Rd with their mouths full of either lollies, bags of sweets, or frozen chocolate bars. Innocence at its best!

When Melinda's children had grown up and were all now residing in South Wales, she would often send them to a similar village shop called Allsorts, and ask them to get her a 50p mix-up of similar sweet confectionery. She was still a big kid at heart, looks can be deceptive! Ask any pensioner what their preferences were in the sweet range, somehow we would all be surprised.

With Sid's parents' shop being a tobacconist as well as selling confectionery and many grocery items, cigarette sales were popular amongst some of the schoolchildren. Not really allowed to smoke cigarettes as minors, their pocket money was sometimes spent on them, for their own personal use. Not having enough pennies to purchase a pack of five cigarettes, usually the Woodbine brand, Sid would open up a sealed packet and sell them one single stick cigarette. Illegal as far as the law was concerned, but those who knew had never mentioned the sales to the adults or anyone else. It had been an ongoing secret known to many in and around the neighbourhood.

Not that the adults, or parents in most cases, were stupid; they were well aware of their offspring entertaining the odd cigarette or two, but hoped that it wouldn't become a permanent habit in later years. Melinda, with the fear of fire, matches and cigarette lighters included, had always abstained from the nicotine stick. Others, some for purely personal reasons, included purchasing a single cigarette from Sid's parents' shop rather than feeling left out of the 'gang', so to speak. Fear of saying no and being ostracised from them, had them smoking the cigarette whether they'd wanted to or not.

Certain that her siblings had smoked cigarettes as children, Melinda's late husband was also a regular at Sid's when a young child. She'd not known him properly at the time, known of him but hadn't actually met and socialised with him. He was a regular at her dad's barber shop from an early age, so his face was familiar in the neighbourhood. Being four years younger, Melinda and Peter's paths hadn't crossed back then.

With parents who had all smoked cigarettes, and cigars occasionally, during their early years and beyond, they'd no valid reason to exercise rights to their offspring; deferring them from the habit-forming cigarette, and they hadn't. In hindsight, a quiet talk to them could have put them off, but children had a mind of their own and would either abstain or join in with their friends, their choice.

Today, the expense along with the health risks, all now too apparent regarding cigarette smoking, had plenty of people giving up the habit. Places prohibited from smoking had also forced the issue there, all good in retrospect. With many cancer-related diseases attributed to the contents of a cigarette, nicotine primarily, though not always the reason for death; prevention has become paramount and the once popular lit stick protruding from people's mouths, is no longer quite so favourable.

Melinda was glad she'd not entertained the habit as a child, though chance would have been a fine thing! She'd still managed to contract breast cancer in her fifties, proving that cigarette smoking hadn't caused it, hers anyway. Sadly, Peter had passed away from lung cancer, a more than possible reason that smoking had triggered the disease. Not proof, but a definite source of probability, with confirmed facts to back up logic and the breathing issues relating to it.

Sid was a well-remembered character, a 'Granville' of Open All Hours, so to speak. A popular TV situation comedy of years ago, one recalled with humour and a wry smile; Sid had never had a girlfriend though, not as far as Melinda could recall, unlike Granville. Likeable for all the right reasons, the said shop and its memories will never fade, not from Melinda's mind.

Next door to Sid's was the dairy shop, delicatessen, and fresh food retailers, of sorts. The middle-aged couple, when Melinda was a schoolgirl, that was, were lovely people; helpful, courteous and so contented, running their establishment. Smiles were constantly on their faces. Fresh cow's milk, in glass bottles then, was a major purchase, along with slices of breaded cooked ham, cut from the bone; cut whilst customers watched and licked their lips. Bought in amounts required, enough to fill their family's appetites, and weighed on the shop scales to secure a price. Served with mashed potatoes and sliced tomato, a meal with breaded cooked ham was lapped up for an evening.

Sliced beef, tenderly cooked with succulent juices, chicken, turkey and the like; fresh cream and rich butter, cheddar cheese cut to size and humongous pork pies sat in the cool cabinet. The shop's owners would cut a slice and, like the ham on the bone, weigh it to provide a price to the customer. Served with sweet pickles and either mashed potatoes or fried chips, a more than substantial meal was provided without too much preparation. An alternative pie, used similarly, was the pork and egg pie, sliced to the customer's choice and thickness. Single rashers of bacon were sold, just enough to whet purchaser's appetites, and easy on the pocket of hard-working families.

Melinda had bought the odd pint or two of milk to drink on the way home from school there, but her real recollection of the lovely couple had come later on in life, as a married lady with two small children. Volunteering to collect monies from houses for the Football Pools, along with their guessed entries to football matches yet to be played, she would knock on the back entrance and spend a while listening to their conversation, with interest. Sometimes a cup of tea was accepted if Melinda's round was almost completed. Then elderly, they so loved company after the shop had closed permanently, and would undoubtedly have passed away today.

Melinda's nan's sterilised milk had come to mind when thinking about the occupants of the now closed and boarded up retail shop with living premises at the rear, a dairy product sold in the small popular outlet then. Cooked beetroot had also nudged her brain, a product cooked by the couple themselves and sold in the shop to customers. Freshly cooked produce grown in their back garden and, as she recalled, delicious in taste. Eggs, a staple food of the era and of today, were required by all neighbourhood families; sold in boxes of six and were replaced quickly as supplies had run down.

The other remaining shops in the vicinity had eluded Melinda's mind, unsure as to what they had actually sold; obviously, not establishments she had entered often, or indeed at all. There were only two other retail shops before the end of St Lukes Rd, leading onto York Rd, a busy main road.

Melinda's memory hadn't been that clouded, not really; they could well have been empty premises!

With the primary school opposite, her memories were good in her years there. Good years and innocence, all that childhood had entailed!

Chapter Nine

St Lukes Rd Primary School, a place Melinda had attended from the age of four until the beginning of her secondary years of education. A building full of history and mystery; an older structure used for its purpose for years and years, educating the children of Totterdown. Melinda had loved going there and learning in her early years.

Most of the children from St Lukes Rd and the neighbouring streets had attended the school, along with sibling after sibling as they were born to parents of larger families, the majority in Melinda's childhood. Classes had included an older sister, whilst another class would occupy her younger brother, and so on, and so on.

At one stage in Melinda's early years, all four of her siblings had attended there, along with families of five or more children in her street. Annual school photographs hadn't just included the children of the class year, but also a separate photograph of siblings educated in the building, all at the same time.

Needless to say, the neighbourhood had consisted of families becoming familiar and friendly with one another, an ever-growing population in one small area of the country. A dot on the landscape, so to speak, where lives were shared and almost everyone around had known someone in the families of the houses around about. Strangers in Totterdown! What were they?

An open book community; if you wanted to keep a secret from somebody nearby, chances are that someone somewhere would get wind of it, and the secret would be leaked to others in the close-knit vicinity. Gossip of sorts, but Totterdown was renowned for families helping one another when needed, animosity a minor friction amongst all concerned.

Likewise, children mixed with other children, visited each other's houses after school and at weekends, and, as they entered the 'big' school became paid babysitters for the smaller beings of the community. Allowing parents a well-deserved break in one of the local public houses for an evening, all had worked out perfectly, and teenage babysitters were familiar and well-trusted to care for their younger offspring.

Had there been a few close encounters over the years? Of course, there had. Bonfire night being a firm favourite there. Pinching contents of wood to burn on the day, from one pile to another. Where gangs in Victoria Park were concerned, frequent fights and a few bruised bodies had occurred along the way. Just one example that Melinda could remember, though there were plenty of others during her childhood. Children will be children and tempers flared, but as quickly as they had fired up, their friendship was repaired again, all forgotten in an instant.

The school was managed by several schoolteachers, male and female. Melinda hadn't much recollection regarding her teachers in her younger years; at four years old, her class teacher's name had eluded her. It would have been Miss or

Sir, surnames weren't always added to the end. Had Melinda been a good pupil? Yes, at first she'd hardly uttered a word whilst in class. Quiet and shy, sometimes to the extreme, she would listen intently to the teacher and take in as much as her little brain could handle.

A slimly built child and small in height in comparison to others in her class, Melinda had been completely happy at being a member largely unnoticed. Not indifferent to others there, the children that had stood out from the crowd had received much more attention from the adults there. Normal was okay as far as Melinda was concerned, and she'd plodded on with school and schoolwork at her own pace.

Average, Melinda's marks were; nothing had stood out regarding her primary education, on either a good or a bad note. She'd done the best she could and knew that she couldn't have improved on what she had actually achieved, a scholar through and through. Not the top of the class, or indeed the bottom (the dunce of the class), Melinda had shrugged her shoulders knowing that bettering her score was near impossible, and she was content with her lot.

Melinda hadn't mixed much in the playground and would sometimes settle into a corner with one of her classmates, or alone with a book. The space outside wasn't huge; more than enough for the little beings and bigger children to vent out their energy though, in between learning subjects required by the board of education. Skipping, hop scotch, and racing one another from one end of the outside space to the other; pupils were creating play and sharing energy whilst outside of the classroom.

Memories of one sunny day during school time, Melinda's vivid recollection of a white t-shirt and a brightly coloured flared skirt, decorated with yellow and white flowers on a black background, had her recalling being stung by the biggest bumble bee she had ever seen; a memory of an event, an occurrence as if it was only yesterday.

Her hands were placed in the material of the swinging skirt, and, whether the bumble bee had mistaken the pattern of the flowers on the piece of clothing as real, who knew? The black and yellow striped insect had stung a finger on her hand, as she'd moved it, and tears had fallen with the extreme pain it had dealt her.

The school nurse in attendance had relieved the sting with the 'blue bag', a tried and tested way of deadening the pain. Wrapped inside a small white sock, the 'blue bag' remained on the appropriate finger for ages, until she'd felt better. Melinda's mum and nan had sworn by the 'blue bag' of the day, and although no other repercussions of the incident had arisen, she'd not liked the flowered skirt after that, the fear of replicating the experience foremost in her thoughts. Today, wasps and bees always had her running for cover. Dodging and diving to avoid the little 'buggers', annoying little things. She'd much prefer spiders!

With the school building being an old structure, rumours of the ghost of a small child known as the 'blue boy' running up and down the back stairs, behind the classroom used for science lessons and creative art, were rife. Melinda had made papier mâché models with her classmates there. Team efforts that were marked accordingly, by the teachers, after precision and student detail to accuracy on a particular topic had been set to them.

Many pupils, however, were more interested in opening the door to the set of stairs, than in the classroom project at the time, in search of the resident ghost. Aptly named for the blue outfit of olden years that he had worn, somebody must have espied his image somewhere along the road. As the teacher had walked out of the room into the adjacent classroom, leaving the pupils unsupervised temporarily, certain youngsters would quickly peer up the stairs in the hope of seeing him, before the teacher's presence had returned.

Some claim to have seen him and had become frightened after the event, but Melinda had never experienced catching sight of him; she had stood at the bottom of the stairs in hope though, admittedly. Nevertheless, when asked to work in the classroom itself, apprehensive children would become a little unnerved at being there. He hadn't caused anyone any harm there, none at all. Sadly, the 'blue boy' has gone forever, with the school building being demolished in the 1970s in favour of a commercial building that had made spices; an establishment known as Bart Spices. The area around the school is now an industrial site for various different outlets, creating employment for people living in the neighbourhood.

Melinda's sister, Melanie, now a mere sixty years of age, works in the cafe part of Fowlers Motorcycles, a business that has lasted longer than many others around. Going back to her roots, so to speak, Melanie wasn't a stranger to Totterdown and her memories of St Lukes Primary School would be similar to her older sister's, Melinda.

Melinda's teacher in her final year at St Lukes Primary School, was the son of the famous Harry Dolman, a chairman of Bristol City Football Club between 1949 and 1974. He designed the first set of floodlights installed at Ashton Gate stadium in the early 1950s and was fundamental in the design and build of the Dolman Stand, which opened in 1970 at the cost of £235,000. In 1974, having deposed as chairman, he took on the presidency which he held until his death in 1977, aged eighty. His wife, Marina, held the position after that.

Mr Dolman (his first name was Tony, Melinda recalled) or Sir, as she knew him, had taught the class that prepared itself for the 'big' school, the comprehensive education after the primary years.

As quiet as Melinda was, her marks were good and, with his help, she moved on to St George's Grammar School the following year. A step up from the comprehensive, he'd reckoned that her learning skills and intelligence were in line with the grammar schools and their educational curriculum.

Melinda had never really excelled in anything, unlike her youngest sister who was a noticed pupil throughout her childhood, but hadn't argued; not a teacher's pet, by any means, she'd done as she was told and continued her education in the same fashion until leaving school at fifteen years of age.

The Banana bridge, or Langton Street bridge, opposite the school, with York Rd on one side and Clarence Rd on the other, is a pedestrian access for people in the neighbourhood. Shaped like a curved banana, it has, over the years, been painted a dark green and a bright yellow; typical colouring of bananas themselves, ripening to ripe. The early English name for Bristol was 'Brigstow', the place of the bridge, and in all, there are nineteen to see.

A local icon in Bristol, Grade 11 listed, as it's been around for donkey's years, to Melinda and the neighbourhood it was and still is, a means of crossing the river to get to the other side and wherever you were headed at that precise moment in time. She would cross it daily when beginning on the employment ladder, various jobs worked in the vicinity.

Have legs, will travel; a saying of the day. Buses and cars were only used where essential. If you could manage the journey on foot, then that's what people of all ages would do. Reliance on transport was always secondary to requirements. Salaries wouldn't stretch to luxuries, as a rule; that's what they were in Melinda's childhood, luxuries.

Recalling crossing the bridge with her friends from school on an evening and weekend, on occasion; an old black-and-white photograph had somehow come out of the woodwork of recent years, on the social media page of mobile telephones. Four girls walking across the banana-shaped bridge, unknowingly being snapped by someone.

Melinda had been looking towards the floor, head bowed. She'd recognised herself by the blue and white striped dress she had been wearing, and the short, barber shop hairstyle. Probably around ten or eleven years of age, the three other girls were as surprised as she was when espying the image on the Facebook media. What had Melinda looked like? A cringeworthy face had appeared. She'd virtually lived in the dress in the 1960s, and what had her dad thought, where cutting her hair was concerned?

The bridge had also held sad reminders, as well as obscure ones. A laugh had erupted remembering her dad's motorbike and sidecar, and his regular visit to The Mitre public house on the other side of the bridge, for a few alcoholic beverages. On one occasion, after driving the vehicle to the establishment and parking it outside, the motorbike and sidecar had been stolen and disappeared. Walking home, a disgruntled Thomas had later found it, complete with numerous empty bottles of beer inside. A joyride with a difference. He was not amused!

Peter's (Melinda's late husband) aunty had jumped from the bridge to her death when in her later years. A widow with adult children and grandchildren, she had walked down St Lukes Rd, crossed over the road onto the bridge, and jumped into the water. A lovely lady, lonely in her own home, she had exorcised her own wishes. A single shoe remained on the bridge afterwards and was picked up later. Aunty Florence would be remembered for all the good things about her, but the recollection of her demise could never be forgotten.

Peter's aunty wouldn't have been the first person to end up in the river crossing the bridge, and probably not the last, either. The murky water wasn't an invitation to swim in it, unfortunately, blue wasn't a colour that Melinda would describe the contents of the river, more a dark and dirty grey. Definitely not Mediterranean colours in beautiful pictures in magazines.

Only a few minutes' walk from Temple Meads railway station, the location held visitors' interests. To Melinda and others in the neighbourhood, the bridge was a means to an end, and probably still is today. She'd revelled in walking the wobbly suspension bridge in the Yukon when visiting Canada and Alaska when older, but the Banana bridge had held no such experience; a grade 11 listed construction, the bridge had remained a part of her childhood and nothing more.

Chapter Ten

Walking along York Rd itself, Melinda had remembered the church, St Lukes Church, and having been christened there with the elder of her two sisters and a brother; a triple celebration, of sorts. The youngest two siblings have never gone through the ceremonial occasion. The church, along with the school, are long gone now, bulldozed into dust to allow commercial buildings and estates into the free space. Melinda's only recollection was that of her and two siblings being christened there, an image on the social media page would enhance her thoughts, but honestly, it was all a bit of a blur.

The road carried on to Bedminster, turning left, and Temple Meads railway station on turning right. Bedminster was a hub of shopping outlets and housing for the working-class community. The Redcliffe bridge led to Redcliffe hill and St Mary Redcliffe Church, and then into town, the centre of Bristol. So many areas had changed over the years, and not always for the better.

Melinda used to cross the Banana bridge, walk through the garden area of the high-rise flats opposite and finish up at the church, St Mary Redcliffe Church; a short-cut to her work buildings. There had been a few she'd been employed in that were within walking distance, and she had known the short cuts to all of them.

Walking down memory lane, so to speak, Melinda headed back up St Lukes Rd on the opposite side of the road that she'd walked down. How that side had changed over the years; a catastrophic consequence of things gone awry. A development process disastrously upsetting the apple cart in days gone by. Old photographs of the road confirmed the destruction of a part of Bristol that had been functioning perfectly well beforehand. If it's not broken, then don't fix it! One of Melinda's favourite expressions.

The outside wc/public toilets as such, next to the school and constructed of brick and the like, were there to see in the corner; just before entering the railway bridge tunnel. Equipped with the necessary facilities for both male and female passersby, the building had had good use over the years. Today, the corner of the road is just that, a corner of the road.

Needless to say, some had used the building to smoke a crafty cigarette out of eyesight, though not in Melinda's case (she'd never smoked). After purchasing a single nicotine stick from Sid's parents' shop, the wc was a convenient stop on the way home from school for some of the schoolchildren. They hadn't done any harm to anyone, not really.

Going back under the tunnel and out the other side, the only visible construction remaining were the 99 steps leading to Richmond Street at the very top. Where terraced houses had used to be, full of families living in the community, happy and contented, the pavement and grass verge was all that now remained. Sadly, in years gone by, the council had knocked down the wrong houses; they should have demolished the houses on the Victoria Park side of the road!

As a result, all houses on both sides were destroyed. What a complete and utter waste of residential properties in the area. Older properties tend to equip themselves with character, as opposed to the 'boxes' of today. Melinda much preferred the older buildings and her residence today was built in 1905, a stone-built semi-detached property. Not the Ritz, but home for her, and somewhere she was comfortable with.

Thomas's barber shop, well it had belonged to his boss really; he was merely an employee at the time. That building had been demolished too, a first foot on the ladder for Melinda's dad, leading to the purchase of his own shop directly opposite, later on; namely 51 St Lukes Rd. The small church had gone as well, now occupied by two residential properties.

Open spaces were okay, but where a community had pulled together beforehand, with commercial properties, shops and housing, there was now a void; an empty space of silence. The price paid for the future wasn't always a good thing, and Totterdown was one area that was evident. Cramming high-rise apartments on a small piece of land wasn't always the answer to the housing crisis and the increase in population, not that Melinda's thoughts would ever be acknowledged.

Crossing the small road leading to Windsor Terrace, Pylle Hill Crescent and various other side streets leading up to Totterdown's part of the Wells Rd, stood the Cumberland public house once ran by the same couple for decades. Pylle Hill Crescent appears to have a historical meaning; the Saxon Charters of Somerset used the word 'pyl' as the name for a stream or brook and as Totterdown was part of Somerset in Saxon times, it may be that it was the springs on the east slopes of Pylle Hill or the stream that once ran on the line of what is now St Lukes Rd that gave Pylle Hill its name.

The male owner, or landlord, was called Stanley and his daughter's name was Angela. Sadly, the lady landlord's name had eluded Melinda for the moment, and as Amelia, her mum, was no longer around, she hadn't been there to ask. Something at the back of her mind had registered her name beginning with a 'C'. The public house had had a lot to tell, things Melinda could laugh about today. Secrets of the past are now brought to the surface, so to speak.

Amelia had worked as a cleaner in the Cumberland for years, and living directly opposite was a definite advantage. She could fall out of bed and into work, theoretically! The landlords were familiar with the children and when Melinda had progressed in age, to seventeen to be exact, they had allowed her into the public house to partake in a drink or two; with or without a boyfriend in tow.

Not looking the age she was, she'd found it difficult to get into anywhere that teenagers and nearly adults had entertained themselves. As trusted occupiers of the public house, Melinda had known not to misbehave on the premises and didn't. Her parents wouldn't have been happy bunnies if she had, for certain.

Whilst engaging in a date there once, with a boy she had fancied for ages before linking with, she'd met with an obscure but now laughable experience, one similar to a comedy scene on the TV today. When heading for the ladies' toilets, she'd been approached by an old schoolfriend; she hadn't seen him for years, though he had still lived locally. He had asked her out on a date, knowing full well that she was there with a boyfriend at the time.

A second visit to the ladies' conveniences had yet another encounter in the hallway, an unknown gentleman had approached her, well not completely unknown if she was honest. He was a regular visitor to the fish and chip shop she had worked in on weekends; one that was usually inebriated after several pints of beer throughout the evening. He was asking Melinda for a future date and appeared completely sober this time.

Walking back to the table she had been sitting at with the date of the evening, a current boyfriend of a few weeks or more, a chuckle emerged from Melinda's mouth. She had declined both offers on the day, but in years to come had actually married the latter of the advances. How things had materialised, in a local public house of no significance, was unforeseen on the day. Melinda hadn't favoured him that much then.

The Cumberland had become a regular for a while until she'd reached eighteen years of age and was legally allowed to partake in other premises; there was one other venue Melinda had managed to get into though, a place known as the PMP club, running a small hotel along with a weekly disco venue on a Thursday evening for the locals.

The PMP club was in Bedminster, next to the church and opposite a small public house called the Apple Tree. Not much space as an established place to drink, the regulars partaking in a cider or two would visit it often. Equivalent to supping alcohol in your front living room, Melinda hadn't ever been inside to have a drink, merely glanced through the open door.

Melinda would pay a visit to the PMP club, usually on a weekly basis with a boyfriend, and becoming familiar with those that had also attended had helped her no end, in the long run. Still only seventeen years of age, she'd decided to end the relationship with her boyfriend at the time, and after he'd walked out of the hotel and the disco, Melinda had asked one of the boys there to get her a drink from the bar. She'd handed him the monies applicable to purchase the alcoholic beverage required.

A tad cheeky, Melinda had realised, but Peter and his gang of mates were now there, the gentleman who had approached her in the Cumberland. How Melinda had walked over to him and asked if he still wanted to date her, she'd not known, but that was exactly what she'd done; a shy, naive girl had suddenly grown a backbone and their marriage had lasted forty-three years, until his sad death at sixty-six years of age.

Melinda had smiled to herself whilst remembering the PMP hotel, a building now long gone; a city farm, namely Windmill Hill City Farm, now stood there, a place for city schoolchildren to visit the animals and creatures usually resident in the countryside; in the lush green fields visible from certain angles of Bristol. Sheep, cows, pigs and chickens; general common birds and animals, but there had, over the years, been much rarer animals for children to see and be educated about. Gone was the hotel, but not Melinda's memories of the place; they would never ever fade.

Recalling the Cumberland once again, there had been many a celebration in the upstairs room of the public house, Melinda and Peter's wedding reception for starters; after a ceremony in St Michael's and All Angels Church not too far away. A reason to party and drink alcoholic beverages with them becoming a couple. Not the Ritz, but as precious an establishment to celebrate with family and friends. An occasion to remember with pure happiness, one of many, especially now.

Melinda and Peter had celebrated their engagement, along with her eighteenth birthday, in the room above the bar in the Cumberland, too. Her recollections of that occasion were something she'd preferred to forget and not because of the reasons for celebration. Not used to drinking alcoholic beverages to excess, it had been one occasion where she'd not heeded her own warnings.

After leaving the public house and continuing the celebrations at Peter's eldest sister's home, the bathroom was a room she had constantly visited throughout the rest of the evening; finally emptying the contents of her stomach into the toilet bowl. Melinda had collapsed beside it, so ladylike, not! The quiet and naive person who usually remained in the background had suddenly become a spectacle for all to ogle at; something Melinda hated then, and even now. What a state she was!

The only other occasion she could recall, thinking back, where alcohol consumption had taken over and portrayed Melinda as a drinker, was all to do with her sister, Melanie. Unknowingly to her, Melanie had spiked her soft drinks with alcohol at a party at her sister's house. Melinda's mind had become nonsensical, talking gibberish and acting a fool. Not that she could remember it herself, all the details in full that was. Peter, Melanie and others there, had filled her in on everything that had occurred in her out-of-character state of mind.

The next day effects of excessive drinking were not good, her head banging and throbbing, along with everyday activities left until sober. Not a nice feeling at all, and something she'd preferred not to make a habit of, or repeat and experience again. Never say never, but a willing participant Melinda wasn't.

Thomas, Melinda's dad, was a regular customer in the bar, Sunday afternoons becoming normal hours to partake in a pint or two; whilst Amelia was cooking the Sunday roast for the family of seven. With his presence back home, becoming later and later, Thomas's wife was not amused. Cooking a roast dinner was never a simple affair, taking hours rather than minutes out of a busy day.

On one specific Sunday, she had carried the prepared dinner across the road, over to the Cumberland public house, complete with knife and fork, and deposited the contents at his larger-than-life figure. Embarrassment overload or what?

Whether he'd continued his Sunday beverages in the public house after the event, Melinda couldn't quite remember. The visual image of her mum's actions often caused hysteria in her mind, though. What the other loyal customers had thought at the time, could only be guessed. Only Fools and Horses had come to her head, a typical scene involving Del Boy and Rodney; a TV series that had all in stitches of laughter with their antics. Maybe Thomas and Amelia could have earned themselves a few 'bob' with the idea!

Now known as the Star and Dove, and producing meals for the fit and healthy, upmarket food with upmarket prices, a public house so unlike it was in Melinda's day. A sign of the times, she'd supposed.

Chapter Eleven

Victoria Park, the open space near Melinda's childhood home, was more than just a mere park; it had represented living in the past decades and was crucial for many residents in the area. More than just a playground and grassy area for children to release their pent-up energy, one way or another, but much more!

With several entrances and exits, to and from the park itself, it was a shortcut into workplaces for many. Melinda had walked through there after disposing of her children, in creche and primary school. A less lengthy way of reaching the road required, St Lukes Rd as it happened to be, to begin work not too far away. She had lived merely minutes from her childhood home when in her twenties, and in her eyes the residential area was good and familiar.

Returning after a few hours of work, she'd only worked part-time hours at the beginning, via the same route and in time to pick the children up and return home; spending precious hours with them before preparing the evening meal for when Peter had finished his shift at work and ventured back home.

As a teenager, she had walked through Victoria Park on her way home from work when visiting the bank in

Bedminster, and on several other occasions throughout her earlier years. Thomas had advised, no, told Melinda not to walk through there in the dark, but being a teenager who knew better, she hadn't listened. What her dad didn't know, hadn't mattered, in theory; the mind of an adolescent taking no notice of the older generation. Sadly, Melinda wasn't the only one to copy her actions, there were many residents in the neighbourhood doing exactly the same thing. Youngsters pretending to be adults, as the saying goes.

Melinda had halted the shortcuts after a scare one night, one she'd kept a secret for over four years. The park hadn't frightened her at all, but when the darkness had descended, it was the road she had walked after that; a fair bit longer, but definitely safer. Dad hadn't needed to know!

As children, Melinda and her siblings would play near the wall, until Amelia had called them for tea. Not directly in sight of the house, but a minute's walk away. They'd been trusted to stay in that precise part of Victoria Park, not straying any further. Friends would be there too, a hub for children of St Lukes Primary School and local residents' offspring.

Coming back with dirty knees, bruised parts of the body and scratches to the skin; childhood as it used to be. Melinda's son had been thrown over the handlebars of his BMX bike, in Victoria Park, whilst out with his school friend. An accident on his part and obvious bumps and bruises resulting from the occurrence, his friends' mother had dressed his 'baddies' and returned him home, along with the damaged bike. Families looking after families, that was Totterdown then.

With a medically run-down son, after the event, he had contracted German measles and a throat infection; his immune system was at an all-time low and he'd picked up everything going around. A mild dose of scarlet fever, if Melinda had recalled correctly, was also caught. Such a sorry sight, but children are normal children, all said and done.

The playground was there, equipped with several swings, a slider, a roundabout and a climbing frame. There for mothers to take the youngest members for play on the ground equipment. Catching fresh air and a few hours, or less, outside of the house. Playtime with the little darlings and a chance to breathe, outside a housewife's routine and general day-to-day activities. A housewife's work is never done; how true was the saying!

A change is as good as a rest; another saying so, so true. The smiles on their adorable faces were infectious, enjoying being outside in the sunshine, fresh air, whether warm or cold; their mothers would smile too, just watching them. All wasn't doom and gloom at all, just ask the children (the younger ones).

Further on through the park itself, was St Mary Redcliffe Primary School; there for the many children born and living around Totterdown. After St Lukes Primary School had closed for good, after being demolished in favour of commercial buildings being erected, it was St Mary Redcliffe Primary School that the remaining children of primary ages were placed.

Melinda herself had already moved to St George's Grammar School by then, so the upheaval hadn't affected her at all. Location-wise, St Mary Redcliffe Primary School was ideal, nearer than St Lukes School from Melinda's home. Parents had opted for St Lukes initially, the alternative having restrictions for entry, some most parents hadn't qualified for.

Regular churchgoers were one stipulation, as Melinda had recalled, but with St Lukes closing, the criteria had changed, and all pupils were allowed to be educated there.

With parts of the educational building being in Victoria Park itself, the views from the classroom windows were good, scenic and pleasant. No brick walls to look out at, or busy roads; a recreational area inside of a recreational area, so to speak! All good for the children. Melinda's siblings had been required to adjust to a new school and new teachers, and adjust they did, admirably so.

Teachers will say that they have no favourites in their class, but that wasn't always the case. Mr Bishop, aka Sir, Melanie's teacher, had a soft spot for his pupil, without a doubt. Having been mistaken for Melanie throughout her younger years, and vice versa, the said teacher had picked Melinda up and turned her around whilst walking with Amelia. Melinda had had no clue as to who the gentleman was, and a bemused grimace was shown on her face. Mr Bishop was left red-faced afterwards. Was Melanie a model pupil? Probably not, but she was obviously a classroom pupil he had liked whilst she studied there.

Melinda's younger sister was always a hit with the teachers in St Mary Redcliffe Primary School. With a photographic memory and an intelligent mind, she was sought out for her higher-than-normal class results for a child of her age. A child prodigy, no, but a credit to the school and its teaching abilities. Was she a brain surgeon now? Absolutely not, but of the five siblings, it was Melinda's youngest sister who had shone on the education front.

The road leading to the park gate, past the school, was one walked by parents and children alike; and by adults taking a shortcut home from their place of work. She had used the road a lot when working in the vicinity, and when wanting to shop in Bedminster for groceries and whatever else was required on a day-to-day level.

Whilst living in the area with Peter and the children, young children at the time, Saturday's had become a regular walk through the park to the shopping area; with a break on the way back for the children to play. Stephanie's buggy would be laden with shopping bags full of groceries, there to feed the family for the whole week. As she got out of the buggy to play, the bags of food would topple to the ground with a bang. The weight of her body had held the bags in place, freeing Melinda from carrying them as well as pushing her daughter home.

Peter and Melinda did have a car at the time, but they had legs too, and the weekly shopping was done on foot. Peter would visit his dad whilst the groceries were being purchased and she would join him, with the children, afterwards. Saturday was family day when the siblings would meet up at their dad's home for a chip shop meal. Routine at its best. Family being so important.

Along Hill Avenue, another road circling Victoria Park was a garage for the repair of motor vehicles and a few other small shops selling their wares; all mainly situated at the end of one of the smaller streets leading from St Johns Lane to Hill Avenue. There was a busy grocery cum off-licence, and above the door, the proprietor's name was shown. Mr and Mrs Pickles had occupied the establishment for years and were popular residents in the area.

A shop well equipped with groceries and alcoholic beverages, and more importantly, open later into the evening.

There for forgotten items whilst doing the weekly shop, or something used prior to its nominated time. Melinda had reserved one morning each week to bake and cook meals for the family. Minced beef and onion pies marked with days from Sunday to Saturday and put into the freezer until that day had arrived. Quiches, coconut rock cakes (Peter's favourite) and other pastry-based foods to last throughout the week.

Missing one item in the kitchen cupboard had often caused Melinda to visit Pickles' store for that all-important ingredient, to complete the week's meals well in advance. Money was tight and budgeting was a necessity, then and now. That one ingredient had probably cost a few pence more than the supermarket in Bedminster, but, when needs must!

Being opposite one of the gates to the entrance of the park had also prompted the shop to become a meeting point, a place for teenagers to congregate, for several different reasons. Gangs of youngsters would be seen there, their bums parked on the stone wall. Smoking crafty cigarettes and supping cans of beer and lager, whether of age or not.

Apart from the obvious noise at times, they'd done no harm to anyone, and Mr Pickles would be outside the shop door at regular intervals, keeping an eagle eye on them if he'd thought that anything sinister was occurring. A meeting point it was, primarily, and nothing more. Melinda was sure that the proprietors would be at their parents' doors if required, with any bad news of teenagers behaving badly! Totterdown it was, all said and done.

Benches were placed around the grassed areas, under trees and along the paths, too many to count. Places of seating there for relaxing, watching offspring play and kick a ball about, or just resting their bodies. A quiet chat amongst friends, reading a paperback in peaceful solitude, or just relieving their brains of day-to-day activities for a few minutes, or more. A recreational park it was when required to be so. School, short cuts aside, Victoria Park was an essential part of Totterdown and Bedminster, and always will be.

The church Melinda and Peter had married in was accessible from Victoria Park; another entrance to and from people's residences, and the shortcut way to Melinda's aunt, uncle and elderly grandmother. Initially, Nan, as she was known, had resided next door to her and her family, but when the hardware shop had been sold it was Melinda's aunt Evelyn and uncle Bill who had taken her in. The apartment above the shop had belonged to the business and sadly, Nan wasn't allowed to live there anymore. The accommodation had been perfect for her, but things happen and life moves on.

A high-rise apartment block it was, thirteen floors in height. Melinda's relatives had lived on the eleventh floor, their door number being forty-nine. A two-bedroomed accommodation, more than adequate for the three of them to live in comfortably. A balcony, there to admire the view across the city had added fresh air to an otherwise contained building, enough to place a few chairs in when needed.

Melinda would visit her nan, aunty and uncle regularly; with or without her children, and often with her sister, Melanie, and her daughter. At ninety-six years of age, Nan had seen a lot of life, and thirteen children, several grandchildren (too many to mention and recall) and even more great-grandchildren later, her energy level was always good.

Melinda would walk her nan around Victoria Park at ninety-five years young, giving her some exercise and fresh air. She'd loved it, being out in the open. Sadly, at ninety-six she'd fallen out of bed and a few months later had passed away. A lovely lady, who, as she'd aged, had never forgotten Melinda or her children. Not remembering their names (there were a lot of great-grandchildren to recall) at the end, two shiny fifty-pence pieces would be given to Melinda on leaving, to pass on to them when visiting alone. A relative to look up to, and today so sorely missed.

Windmill Hill, as the area was named, was a residential area consisting of high-rise apartment blocks and terraced houses with smallish back gardens to the rear. Set on a hill, the views there were favoured in a large city and appreciated. St Michael's and All Angels Church was nestled down one of the side streets adjacent to the park itself; terraced houses opposite it, and on either side, not set on its own. Melinda had remembered the building well, as well as the local vicar who had married them both at the time.

Chapter Twelve

Melinda and Peter had saved for a whole year for their wedding day. With four younger siblings to keep in food and clothing, paying for their eldest daughter's wedding celebrations was way out of their capability, financially that was, and Melinda had understood that. The harsh 'Do what you want, just don't expect me to pay for it', was upsetting at the time but par for the course where her dad's words were concerned. A 'Congratulations both', would have been all that was needed.

Rent payable to Melinda's dad and to Peter's parents continued whilst a second job, three evenings a week after normal working hours, was done by Melinda. The proceeds were saved separately for the wedding and not once touched or used for anything other than the day itself. Peter was never a saver, before or after their marriage, but Melinda had ensured debts hadn't occurred whilst leading a normal life outside of working hours.

A drive to the seaside on a weekend had included a packed lunch picnic to eat whilst there, and walking along the sandy beach hadn't cost a penny. Admiring the scenery outside of their regular habitat was something memorable, and had whiled away a few hours together without breaking the bank, so to speak. More often than not, Melinda's two youngest siblings would accompany them, The 'Can we come too?' ringing in their ears as they proceeded to leave the front door couldn't be ignored. It wasn't often that they had been refused.

Feeding the ducks in Portishead, just outside of Bristol, had excited both Melinda's siblings and in later years, their own two children. Spending recreational time together didn't require forking out money continuously, and that was something that continued throughout their married life. "Don't fix it if it isn't broken," a phrase so true. "Why buy new when the old one isn't broken? Why spend excessive money when it's not necessary?" The simple life had had a lot to answer for and was something both Melinda and Peter had been more than grateful for.

She'd recalled a conversation whilst on holiday, when a gentleman was putting pressure on Peter to upgrade to a higher-star hotel for the same cost, and had questioned his reasoning as to why he had steadfastly refused the offer.

"Why would I want to leave here and mingle with those above me? The people holidaying here are those living my way of life, a life I love and have no inclination to change. The answer is no, but thank you." The man had left and walked away, with a flea in his ear. Peter was Peter, happy with his lot until his last breath.

Once a week, as a rule, they would visit the public house opposite Melinda's home. A few drinks and mixing with residents of Totterdown for a quiet conversation about something or other. Not gossip, but friendly banter between people of the area; known characters of the local streets catching up with one another. Conversations about work, family members, and sometimes information about elderly residents passing on. Ladies and gentlemen of a certain age leaving their homes through death, rather than moving out of the neighbourhood. Some sorely missed.

A relatively poor area where everybody, well almost everybody, cared about the residents around them. Sometimes, a chat would erupt when a certain person hadn't been seen for a while, and they were concerned. The public house could usually enlighten those unaware, where the elderly had moved away to be with their adult children, unable to look after themselves, or had indeed passed on.

They could also fill in the gaps, where marriages hadn't lasted, and how one or the other of them had conducted an affair with someone else, usually a person in the local area. Widows had remarried widowers or divorcees; single individuals had married childhood sweethearts and schoolfriends from an early age. Gossip of sorts, Melinda had supposed, but life as it was and still is today. Things happen, and life goes on, inevitably.

Peter hadn't been a childhood sweetheart or a school friend. Their paths had crossed at first, when Melinda was only fourteen years of age, even though she'd never acknowledged him or known about it. Thomas would cut his hair in the barber shop, the gentleman's hairdresser, at the front of their living accommodation. She'd never noticed him whilst replenishing her dad's coffee cup, and as far as she could recall, he'd not spoken to her then.

At fifteen, it was the fish and chip shop where she'd worked, that Peter had visited on a weekend. Purchasing food to soak up the beers he had drank whilst in the local public houses. Melinda had laughed at his drunken stupor but hadn't thought past that, not at first. He'd made it obvious that he had liked her, but she'd not ventured further down that road.

At seventeen, Peter had approached her in the public house opposite her residence, and things had progressed from there. She'd not known him around the neighbourhood at all, before then. He had lived within a five-minute walk away, since a young boy, but Melinda hadn't a clue who he was; or known any of his siblings for that matter. Being four years his junior had probably accounted for it, Melinda had said to herself. It was indeed a small world.

It was a lad named David who Melinda was besotted with, one who had lived merely four doors away. Glyn, her friend and former employee from the chip shop had secured a date with him for her. Things began okay on that score, but a relationship between them had fizzled out quite quickly.

They were always friends and remained so until Melinda had grown much older.

Unbeknown to Melinda, Peter had been plying David on their whereabouts whilst they were together, and would turn up, like a sore thumb, with his gang of mates; eagle eyes staring at her all the while. Eventually, Peter and Melinda had ended up together and David was off the scene; as far as romance was concerned. A rather strange meeting up of two soul mates, but the truth, nevertheless. There is nothing so queer as folk, Melinda's nan had used to say. How true that was.

Neither of them had wanted anything fancy for their wedding day. A good day, one to remember, with family around to celebrate with. A dress fit for a queen or princess would have been something Melinda hadn't wanted. A wedding dress, yes. A dress that had done her justice, yes. A dress to celebrate the occasion, yes. An outfit that would cost the earth! Absolutely not. Nice was good enough for her and still is today.

Needless to say, Melinda's dress was pretty and flattering. It was also second-hand and had cost a fraction compared to brand new. Dry cleaned and altered to her satisfaction, she was more than satisfied. Three bridesmaids; Melanie and Melinda's younger sister, along with Peter's niece, all had pretty dresses to suit. All affordable and within budget; their budget.

Peter's mother was unwell, suffering from a terminal condition that would shorten her life, sadly. His father had asked them to remain in his residence, after their wedding. Peter was already there and they had been saving for a deposit for a house at the time, as well as the wedding itself. Melinda had agreed to move in after they were wed; there to help out with both of Peter's parents.

Peggy was determined to be there to see her youngest child, her second son, marry before she had left this earth, and she had. Her figure had lost a lot of weight and being a tall lady, it had highlighted her illness. Nevertheless, she had stood proudly in the church as Peter and Melinda had taken their vows. Smiles adorning her face as the service had continued.

All of her five children were now married and with families of their own, except Peter and Melinda that was. They'd only just started their journey. Only time would tell if they would go on to have children of their own. Nothing was guaranteed, for anyone. The chances of Peggy being there to see any of them were slim, but there was always hope and prayer. A miracle could happen! The wedding had happened almost a year to the day of their engagement. A celebration remembered by all family members there, in St Michael's and All Angels Church in Windmill Hill, followed by a reception and evening do in the public house opposite Melinda's home. No one had to travel too far to witness the marriage or join in the happy event.

The wedding night was spent at Peter's home, Melinda's home now, with both of his parents around. Getting into bed that evening had been eventful, to say the least. Somebody had filled their bed with everything from pairs of boots to items of clothing, and bric-a-brac. Just removing them had had the newly wedded couple in total hysterics.

Peggy had left the reception earlier than most of the other guests, but she'd delighted in the day and headed for home happy and contented. Peter's dad was a man of few words, but he'd appeared to have revelled in the day, not having said that much. Tired or otherwise, Peter's mother was determined to be there for the happy couple. God had granted her wish.

Their honeymoon had begun the following day. Flying from Bristol to Jersey, Channel Islands, a week had been spent cementing their marriage and holidaying abroad for the first time, if you could call Jersey abroad, that was. Being the end of October, the weather was favourable and kind to them. Dry days, though a little cold, the sun had shone for most of the week.

A week later, and they were back to reality. Working for a living and helping to take care of Peggy and Peter's father. Reliant on his wife's household skills; cooking, cleaning, shopping etc., Ernest wasn't familiar with dealing with such things. He had been one of the breadwinners of the century, leaving everything else to Peggy, his wife. She could no longer manage most of the chores. Outside of working hours, Melinda had cooked, cleaned and dealt with everything household related, for the four, and then the three of them. Peggy's guilt at being unable to continue her routine was emotional and heartfelt. Melinda had tried to reassure her that she could take over, but after bringing up five children and taking care of the family of seven, struggling to do anything around the home had left her bereft, and feeling totally useless.

She was unwell, she knew, but her head had wanted to continue her lifestyle, the one she was so used to. It was heartbreaking to see. Melinda had tried so hard to keep her composure, to hold back the tears so wanting to erupt. It was a struggle, but somehow Melinda had remained calm in front of her mother-in-law.

Peggy had passed away just six weeks after their wedding, in her bed at home. The house was missing her dreadfully; she was a well-loved member of the family. A quiet and subdued atmosphere existed for a good while afterwards, all grieving for their family member. Ernest hadn't spoken that much about his late wife and their memories and Melinda had wished that he had, if only for his own sake.

There was a new addition to the family a year later, one Melinda had adopted after finding her sitting on the window sill completely lost. A tiny stray kitten, with black and white markings, and so cute. She became Melinda and Peter's baby until they had children of their own. Ernest, though quiet about the new member of the family, had secretly loved her. He'd not refused her moving in at all.

Melinda's youngest brother had named her Badger, due to her markings, and she had remained with them for fifteen years. Her death was sad, an aged pet loved by the children and adults alike. Melinda had vowed not to have any more pets afterwards, but when her teenage daughter found a kitten across the road from their home, the home Melinda still lived in today, Cleo became an addition to the family.

Cleo was never a replacement for Badger but was equally treated as another child, rather than an animal, a cat. Pets are children in different bodies, all said and done. Who would argue the case? She was a long-haired tabby, Cleo, that was. Twenty years later, Melinda and Peter had lost her, too. Both of them were heartbroken, crying like a baby; their eyes red and swollen with tears, due to their loss. Alone now, Melinda had neither a husband nor a pet. Losing them was far too traumatic.

Repetition wasn't recommended. Melinda's heart wouldn't take it, she knew.

Chapter Thirteen

Melinda's work profile, before and after leaving school was quite lengthy, if she was honest. Not an intellectual person ever, aching to attend university and edging towards a brain surgeon or similar; it wasn't even a consideration. Her head wasn't in the clouds, she convinced herself that she couldn't amount to anything more than working a menial job. *The words director and manager were never to be in her calibre, or so,* she'd thought. Her reckoning on a chosen career, any roads.

It was the Sunday paper round at eleven years of age, followed by serving behind the counter in the local fish and chip shop at weekends; jobs that paid monies before Melinda had actually left school permanently. The fish and chip shop had taught her how to mingle with customers, sort of. Even the inebriated visitors had to be served, one way or another. Peter was one of them and she'd obviously done something right, way back then.

On a rotational basis, Melinda had to clean out the walk-in freezer, a job she had hated doing but had done regardless. The proprietors used to make their own faggots, a popular choice with customers. Served with chips and mushy peas, the meal was a favourite among the residents around the area, mainly the older population.

With frozen blood samples congregating in the freezer, she had been required to remove the spots of blood and other soiled areas until they were clean and dust-free. A repetitive job that had the joints in her body frozen with cold well after she'd finished the chore. Thoughts of being locked in there overnight had had her complete the job in record time, most weeks.

Glyn, her friend and workmate, had often pretended to lock the freezer door and leave her in there. For mere seconds it was, and all in jest, but nevertheless, it was quite frightening. Being a serious, studious child, Melinda had never tried to turn the tables on him when it was his turn to clean the freezer out. Perhaps she should have back then and given him a dose of his own medicine.

Melinda's workmate became a true friend outside of working hours, often inviting her to his home and cooking her a meal. She'd felt like a queen, sat there being waited on hand and foot, and revelled in the experience of being special, something she'd never classed herself as. Glyn had loved cooking and Melinda was someone he could try his meals out on. His mother had worked most days and his twin brother was usually out when she had sampled his cooking.

A movie wanting to watch, but nobody to go with, Glyn had taken her without any ulterior motive. He was more than willing to escort her, as a true friend and nothing more. Clothes shopping was his speciality, where women's outfits and dresses were concerned. Melinda would ask him to go with her, purely for his take on her choices. He was usually right and she had delighted in his company, along with a visit to a coffee shop afterwards.

Glyn was keen on the proprietor's daughter, hankering after her company. They did go out together for a while, but it didn't last. Years down the line, his stance on a permanent relationship had changed from female to male company. Melinda had known, in her heart, his preferences. He was a kind and caring pillar of the community and eventually married another gentleman, living happily until both of their deaths, several years apart.

A best friend of the male kind, Glyn was there for her in her teenage years when needed. Boyfriends had come and gone, but the workmate in the fish and chip shop was always there to listen and lend a shoulder to cry on when wanted. Hormones in teenage years were never predictable, ever. Whoever said that life was easier when younger was indeed cushioned with overprotective parents, or unique in some way.

Melinda's best friend would always be remembered for the good things he had done, the fashion statement he had adorned (standing out from the crowd) and the friendship they had made. Not your normal male teenager hanging out in gangs around the bottom of street corners, smoking crafty cigarettes out of earshot of their parents. Glyn was a gentleman, a caring person and mischievous and witty at times. An all-rounder, some would say and Melinda had been lucky there.

It was one of the inebriated customers that had caught her eye, well the other way around really. She had laughed at his antics, his stumbles across the room and his drunken attempt at making contact with her. The clown of the evening, both

Melinda and Glyn had looked forward to his revisit, a week later, to watch him repeat his performance. Peter was a typical young man and had done no harm to anybody. Enjoying a weekend out with his mates, the excessive drinking wasn't something ventured during the week, a work day.

Glyn's twin brother was drop-dead gorgeous and always acknowledged Melinda when she was at their house. His eyes were on other female ladies around and to him, she was just Glyn's friend and companion, one of many. The impact he'd had on Melinda had etched in her brain, so much so, that she'd promised herself that if she ever had a son of her own, then he would be named Stephen after the gorgeous specimen of a brother that Glyn had.

Melinda's son is indeed named Stephen, she'd never changed her mind. Today, years later, her head would have probably registered a completely different story. He has aged well, deservedly, but isn't the handsome teenager she recalled all those years ago. That image would always remain in her head and Glyn would always be a large part of her teenage years.

Melinda had one other job before leaving school, one that had lasted a whole day! A Saturday job in Woolworths, had her keeping a bay of jumpers tidy for eight tedious hours. Watching customers check out the clothes items and either purchasing them or leaving them there, in an untidy heap; Melinda was in charge of re-tidying them awaiting the next customer's perusal.

Boring, a word that had represented Woolworths employment. She had hated it. Ringing in the next day, she'd advised them that they shouldn't expect her there the following Saturday. Amelia hadn't argued but her dad wasn't a happy bunny.

At comprehensive school, formerly a grammar school, Melinda was at the top of the mainstream class. She was expected to take her O levels at the end of the year, but way back then, once reaching fifteen years of age was allowed to leave school and pursue a career. Abstaining from the examinations was allowed. School qualifications weren't something essential then; a head with common sense was much more apt.

Melinda's head had registered a need to leave school and earn her own money. Paying her way in the family unit was foremost in her mind, back then. With four younger siblings, the finances would be easier if Melinda had managed to obtain a full-time job and contribute. Her beliefs were logical and made sense.

She had checked out the job market first and secured four interviews, being offered each and every one of them. Accepting the one offering the highest salary, she had sheepishly asked to see the school headmaster and informed him of her leaving school for good. He was obviously against her decision, trying to delay the move until after taking the crucial examinations. "She has potential," the headmaster had said. "As a scholar, she could amount to so much more," he had added. Melinda had stood firm though and started work the following week.

Had Melinda made a mistake all those years ago? Who knows! Throughout her years she was rarely out of work. The pay wasn't always brilliant but manageable, bills were usually paid on time. College and university were never something she had hankered for, even now, and she'd always felt her knowledge and intellect would let her down at some stage during the process. Better not to attempt it and fail.

Latin, as a school subject, was never one Melinda had liked or cared about. She'd not needed it and hadn't designs on becoming a doctor or equivalent. Never revising for annual examinations, she'd been pleasantly surprised when the teacher had informed her of her percentage mark. At ninety per cent pass, Melinda had outshone the other schoolchildren there, surprisingly. It hadn't made any difference to her at all and she had dropped the school subject when allowed to do so.

Melinda had made her mind up that she was never going to amount to much, unlike her youngest sister, who was super intelligent and could rule the world. Amelia and Thomas had followed her youngest sister's schooling seriously, but Melinda was just normal, nothing special. She'd convinced herself that doing a menial job in the future was where she stood in life and was to be thankful for it.

Having said goodbye to some of her schoolfriends, there was one who remained a firm friend well after they had both started on the work ladder. After years of absence, finding her on the social media page, they are connected again through the chat line. A person of the past, now living a similar life as Melinda's without any regrets. A friend she was then and a good friend today, whether connecting through chat or in person.

Melinda had started her first job as an office junior in a butter factory. Learning the ropes of a working office, was at first daunting. At fifteen years of age, she was neither a child nor an adult. A shy person who would redden at being spoken to by the boss, she'd had a lot to learn about living.

Melinda was only just getting started.

The office manager, a female lady of a certain age, was a strange person. Not a pretty persona, her facial grimaces were almost always denoting frustration and anger, for whatever reasons. A manly personification with short dark brown hair and a chiselled look on her serious face, Ann wasn't always a pretty sight.

Not a tall person, Ann had disabilities that somehow she had overcome her entire life. Both her arms were shorter than they should be (a birth defect that wasn't something that could be rectified) and sitting down at her desk had been done with unladylike grandeur. Her arms couldn't hold onto the desk, so she would jump onto her chair causing an almighty bang once her bottom had hit the seat of the chair.

Unable to hold a pen or pencil, or use a typewriter, all her correspondence was done via a voice messenger. Letters to be typed were spoken on the messenger and passed on to office staff, Melinda being one of them. Having passed a typing course outside of school hours, Melinda was familiar with the machine and the letter-writing process. Typing was only part, a small part of the job, though.

Learning to answer the telephone had a knack to it, a uniform one that had to be adhered to. A pleasant telephone manner was a must, with politeness always, even if the person on the other end was a little rude and angry. Office staff were trained to be helpful and sincere, whatever the call was about. Ann's deep voice wasn't something she could change, but she did try to sound positive when holding the receiver to her ear with it resting on her shoulder during the conversation. The boss of the butter factory business was a lovely man and he had ensured that Melinda had fitted into the establishment with ease. Ann was Ann, and she had accepted her as part of the office furniture, warts and all. Ann did have a kind heart, somewhere. As a naive teenager, at first, frightened of the Hitler-type persona, she calmed down and got on with the job at hand. That's what she was there for, wasn't it?

There were laughs amid the workforce, those in the office and in the factory itself. As time had gone by, names were put to faces and conversation amongst them had flowed. Melinda was slowly coming out of her shell and she was happy working for a living. The blushes were easing when confronted, but it had taken time.

Every Friday afternoon it was Melinda's job to hand out two packets of the butter, the produce made, to each of the factory staff; their bonus for working hard at ensuring the butter packs were there and available to sell on to establishments, for a profit. Being given the packets of butter had helped their family budget a little and given them a boost throughout their week's hard labour.

The office staff weren't given the butter packets; they hadn't produced the goods so why should they? Melinda or the other staff working in the office hadn't taken umbrage. The factory staff had deserved the free samples and sampling of the goods with their family at home. Ann and her staff were merely administrative employees, keeping the books in order. Hard work, no. Head-work, yes. But fair was fair, and Melinda had proudly handed out the butter to those concerned, with pride.

Melinda had managed the job for almost a year before moving on with her career choices. Another administrative vacancy was applied for and she was offered the post. A vacancy in walking distance from home, saving pennies on bus fare, a definite plus. This time it was located in a paint-producing establishment. Melinda was moving on again and only time would tell whether her stay would be longer than that in the butter factory!

Chapter Fourteen

Melinda's new job was totally different from her previous employment, so different. There was no typing involved and answering the telephone was limited to the odd conversation within the establishment; no outgoing calls whatsoever. She was secretly relieved and wasn't in a permanent panic as to whether she could deal with the incoming call adequately.

Had her confidence improved since leaving mainstream school? Not really, if she was honest. The new job entailed sorting through invoices ready for posting to customers for payment and there were a lot of customers. Paint was a very popular product, apparently. Whether for family houses or industrial use, the various paints made were too numerous to mention. Melinda was gobsmacked at first; paint was paint as far as she was concerned. It was an education in itself.

Melinda and her working partner, a young girl the same age, spent hours placing invoices into envelopes day after day after day. When the pile had been done, all completed, another pile would be placed on their desks and they would start the process all over again. Occasionally, a different task would be given to them, when all invoices had been completed for the month ahead. She, herself, was happy to be given other work to do, but Mary, her working colleague, would have sat at her desk twiddling her thumbs if left to her own devices.

At a certain time of the day, it was Melinda and Mary's job to collect all the posts from each individual office of the establishment, along with other correspondence and parcels from the factory itself. The franking machine was a large and bulky contraption but had served its purpose well. Rather than licking stamps onto each and every piece of post, the machine had done the work for them. Registering weighted parcels for them, the brain wasn't required to ensure the correct postage was put on to it.

A responsible job, nevertheless, Melinda had revelled in the break from folding invoices and placing them in envelopes. A walk around the factory floor and a polite hello from workers there, was sometimes the highlight of the day. Seeing others working hard instilled a reason for the paper invoices, the result of creating the products asked for by loyal customers. All good in the context of things.

Melinda had never really been bored of the job. As long as she was busy doing something, that was enough. Sitting and doing absolutely nothing would have been an entirely different story. She was never good at looking busy when she wasn't; even today, she needed a daily goal to achieve at home. A reason to get out of bed, so to speak. The brain requires motivation even if the body isn't willing. Melinda could try, couldn't she?

The red-faced blushes had emerged yet again. Melinda wasn't seeing enough people to gain any kind of self-confidence in herself. An easy enough job to endure daily, there had been no push to explore her intelligence further. She'd known that but had plodded on, ignoring the fact. It was only when Mary had been interviewed for another job elsewhere, that Melinda had realised that she too had needed to move on and gain some more motivation in any given career.

Their lunch breaks had been taken in the Arnos Vale Cemetery opposite. Sitting on the grass eating their packed lunches, surrounded by graves of loved ones, hadn't caused any concern to either her or Mary. Others were there too, supping up the sunshine in the summer months for an hour out of a nine-to-five mundane job. A peaceful location away from the noise of the factory machines, it was a welcome retreat. The birds tweeting away above them was music to their ears, for that hour of each day in working employment.

Mary had been offered the position she'd been interviewed for and had handed in her resignation at the establishment. She had also informed Melinda that there were other positions available at the retail outlet in the centre of town. Had Melinda been brave enough to interview for one of the vacancies? She was in a dither as she'd decided on whether to take that next step forward.

Macfisheries was a large food retail outlet selling fresh products on a daily basis. Separate counters sold different variations of the same food types. One large counter had concentrated entirely on every fruit and vegetable available in each season of the year and did a roaring trade, very busy all day long. Meals of the day were never ready-made in Melinda's childhood but prepared from fresh by the lady of the household, back in the day.

Another counter had concentrated on fresh fish. The odour radiating from the counter was one of its own, a unique smell only associated with fishermen and their catch. Fish from the sea had filled the entire area, all suitably conveyed in a chilled environment and surrounded by layers of ice to keep the freshness. Whole fish had sat there, unmoving, their eyes staring up at you and mouths wide open. Fish of all variations, some Melinda hadn't known the name of or ever seen before. It wasn't battered cod from the fish shop, was it?

The third counter had been Melinda's favourite. Whole cooked hams sliced to order, cooked beef and succulent chicken; cheeses to die for, from Brie to the everyday favourite, the tasty farmhouse cheddar. Home-cooked faggots, a frequent choice in Melinda's childhood and beyond.

Coleslaw, potato salads and freshly cooked beetroot.

The counter was brimming with delicious mouthwatering meals. Different variations of sausage, pork and beef along with the obscure creations; pork and leek and chorizo, to name just two. The quiche slices were to die for, mouth-wateringly thick and enticing. Melinda's guilty pleasure, if she was honest. Alongside the quiche variations were the large and small pork pies and filled pasties a plenty. Cooked pies and pasties were popular lunchtime snacks, eaten hot or cold. Who wasn't attracted to the delicatessen counter in Macfisheries? Most of the customers had purchased something from there as well as the other two counters. A convenience store with a difference; all was freshly purchased and ready for the housewife of the day to prepare a loving meal for the family of an evening.

The chilled cabinet was there, next to the doors' entrance purposely to lure customers on their hour's dinner break. A quick dash to pick up readily prepared sandwiches, a drink and a snack (something also doubly displayed on the delicatessen counter), before parking their bums on a park bench, back at the office or eating on the go. Tesco's meal deals today could have been invented by Macfisheries back in the day. Nothing had really changed, had it?

Melinda had plucked up the courage to ring the Macfisheries retail outlet and was given an interview date a few days later. She could serve behind the delicatessen counter, couldn't she? Her head had indicated yes but the nerves were getting the better of her as she headed indoors for the confrontation. With her fingers crossed, Melinda had done her best and had hoped, like Mary, she would be successful.

The call the next day had been a good one and she'd passed the interview with flying colours. The fruit and vegetable counter was to be her domain though, not the hoped-for delicatessen area she'd so wanted. Melinda's frown hadn't lasted that long and the new job was a new challenge for her; serving customers in a busy shop had to bring out her confidence and stop the red-faced blushes. Her take on things, anyway. Only time would tell.

Melinda and Mary had started in Macfisheries on the same day and both had immersed themselves into their new employment, initially. Within two months of being there, Mary had become bored and did not adhere to the rules and regulations of the employment contract signed. She was given several chances to conform but had failed miserably, resulting in her notice from Macfisheries itself. Melinda had lost her workmate, even though Mary was never an assistant on the fruit and vegetable counter.

Getting friendly with the regular customers had done what it had said on the tin; it had brought out her confidence when conversing with others. The red-faced blushes were slowly subsiding and Melinda had loved the customer relationship that had resulted over time. A happy face behind the counter was a good morale booster; solemn grimaces from the customers became smiles as they had finished their shopping experience. The job was therapeutic, if not busy; there was no time to dwell on things or any reason to.

There were obviously going to be days where things hadn't gone to plan, many of them. Batches of mouldy fruit had caused an odour on the counter. Melinda would have to sift through the boxes, removing the soft, smelly produce and disposing of the non-sale items in the outside bins quickly. This was done on a daily basis, avoiding costly goods being perished before their time. A time-consuming job but essential when keeping the counter up together and looking pristine.

One situation had come to mind, a laughable one now. Melinda had arrived at work early and was getting the counter ready for the customers before the doors were open to the public. There was an odour, an awful smell coming from underneath, one definitely not associated with rotting fruit and vegetables. An animal scent, a dead body or something similar. Not a good scent at all, absolutely repulsive to the nose.

Hunting all around the area, Melinda had finally found the problem and shrieked aloud. All the staff had stopped what they were doing and suddenly looked her way. The red face had re-emerged, temporarily. Melinda hadn't enjoyed being the centre of attention; it was her worst nightmare. There under the counter was a dead mouse, rotting there in full view. Not a pretty sight at all.

The assistant manager had removed it with a shovel, disposing of it in the outside bin but Melinda had spent the remainder of the day looking for more remains of small rodents, or even live ones come to that. The fear of coming across a mouse or even a rat was consumed in her head for days afterwards. Fresh food and rodents weren't unusual, not really; not something Melinda had wanted to experience again, not in a rush, anyway.

A young lad there, one working on the fresh fish counter, had become friendly with Melinda. Not on a romantic level but as a true friend. They were about the same age and he had a lovely personality. His weight was a serious problem to him; he was on the heavy side. With low esteem due to his stocky build, Dougal (his real name was Ian) had wanted to enrol in a cookery course after work had finished. He'd had aspirations to become a chef somewhere along the line. Melinda had also enrolled in the course and the two of them had caught the bus to the college once a week, after work. The experience was welcomed but there were a few disasters in the making. Her meals hadn't always resulted in being edible. Who had mixed garden peas with mint and chopped onion, anyway? At home, Melinda had merely opened a tin of peas to compliment a meal.

They had both finished the course and Melinda had realised that a career in cooking of any description wasn't on the cards for her, now or in the future. She could burn water if that was possible! The assistant manager had trusted both Dougal and Melinda to prepare a tasty meal in the staff kitchen for all to savour. An eye off of the oven and hob one day had seen the contents of the day burnt to a crisp! He wasn't a happy chappy and needless to say, the trial period had ended badly.

It was back to lunch boxes in their breaks or purchasing goods from the chilled food display. Whether Dougal had gone on to secure a position in the catering industry as a chef, Melinda never knew. It was his dream and she'd truly hoped that he had realised his ambition and lost the excess weight he was trying so hard to eliminate. Stature aside, Dougal was a good person who deserved the best in life.

It was Melanie, Melinda's sister, who had excelled in cooking then and still does today. Peter had always looked forward to her stays when adults. That thick pork chop with perfect crackling was so delicious and Peter had licked his lips afterwards. Melinda had left her sister in the kitchen to her own devices. Getting by was okay, where Peter's wife was concerned and none of the family had ever starved; Melanie's culinary creations had put her to shame, though.

Melanie had been given her orders by Peter when there; his mouth would be drooling over her chocolate cake and cheesecakes. Manchester tart had been one of his favourites or anything coconut related, of the dessert type that was. Coconut-based curries were a definite no-no; Peter was a pie and chips man, all day long.

Both Dougal and Melinda had left Macfisheries employment many months later. Both aiming for pastures new, Melinda's new goal was to return to office-based employment. A job with more regular hours and easier on the feet; the fruit and vegetable shop had amassed hours on her legs, walking up and down the counter continuously.

Nevertheless, Macfisheries had given Melinda the confidence to move on and to converse with others without too many nervous experiences. Her goal had been fulfilled and for that, she was eternally grateful. From not being able to say 'boo to a goose', she could now hold a decent and lengthy conversation with a complete stranger without too much embarrassment.

Where was Melinda heading for next? Her new employment wasn't something her dad was best pleased about. Regardless of his opinions, Melinda began her next venture; something that would take her over two decades of employment with several different companies. Experience was a good thing, along with a good head for certain criteria. Melinda was learning all the time.

Chapter Fifteen

Insurance! Melinda's dad had abhorred insurance and everything it had represented. A rip-off, he would have described the whole business. Mandatory insurance was required to drive a motor vehicle and he'd had no choice but to purchase the same when owning a small car; prior to that, he had owned a motorbike and sidecar, something that had also needed compulsory insurance cover. Anything else was off limits in his eyes, he wasn't wasting his hard-earned cash on covering items in the event of damage; a precautionary measure was just that, a precautionary measure and he wasn't spending money out without some sort of return. Money was stretched to keep the family and there were no arguments there, none whatsoever.

Melinda would have drawn the line at house insurance, a policy designed to replace a family's dwelling in the event of a fire and pay towards renovations if there was a flood or similar catastrophe. There were several exclusions to the cover, admittedly, but it was there to ensure people hadn't remained homeless. The expense had outweighed the eventuality, in Melinda's eyes. He hadn't insured the house itself or the contents, ever. As a family, they were lucky that nothing had happened over the years to cause any major concerns. As young children, at one point, the whole family and their grandfather, Harry, had been forced to live in one room. The roof had obvious leaks and wasn't safe, so cohabiting in the only dry room in the house was unavoidable. The roof was eventually repaired; if insured there could have been funds to complete it earlier, though. Insurance was a pure waste of money in Melinda's dad's opinion so the subject was never spoken about and his hard-earned cash had to be used to repair the damage. It was winter and snow was heavily laid on the ground at the time. It was absolutely freezing, inside and outside.

Life insurance was a definite no-no. Thomas's mind was set and nothing could dissuade him otherwise. On the death of Harry, Melinda's grandfather, it was Amelia, Melinda's mum, who had to find the cost of his funeral with her sister, Peggy. Not exactly having any savings in the bank account, Amelia had used the 'family allowance' (a benefit given by the government to help provide for the children), over several months, to fund her portion of the expenses. Thomas hadn't helped out at all towards burying his father-in-law.

On the day of the funeral, it was Amelia and Sylvia (Amelia's cousin) alone who had attended the occasion. Peggy wasn't well and was unable to be there. A sad occasion for a man who, in later years had lived mainly on the road. He'd deserved more family members there, Melinda had thought, but things hadn't panned out that way.

Critical illness insurance had been there for those wanting to insure against the future of people's health. A policy designed to help pay the bills in the event of losing salaries whilst off sick from work. Thomas hadn't any time for such insurance and had expressed it as useless, not worth the monthly payments asked for. Melinda would disagree; she'd invested in a similar policy for Peter and had been forever grateful when he'd been forced to retire early due to ill health. The monthly pay-out from the policy had definitely helped towards living costs.

Travel insurance wasn't ever thought about. The furthest Melinda and her siblings had gone when younger would have been to family members' houses for a break from the norm. There was one family caravan break she could recall, when older, but Melinda was married with her son on the way by then. Insurance wasn't a necessity.

As years have progressed, insurance is there for almost anything wanted. For a price, a person can insure anything from a pricey piece of artwork to a part of their anatomy. Thomas's reaction today would be laughable and Melinda could see his face there and then; not a happy bunny look, one of disgust had come to mind.

Melinda, at seventeen years of age, was about to embark on a career in insurance. Nothing too exciting at first, she was accepted for a role in a company called Phoenix Assurance, a large building in walking distance from her home. Employed as a filing clerk, the duties weren't that important, not in the world of insurance, that was. She could climb the ladder in time, hopefully. Every morning, Melinda would be handed a pile of posts (correspondence from customers and other insurance companies) and her job had entailed searching for the appropriate file relating to each individual letter amongst the hundreds of files displayed on the shelves at the rear of the building. All supposedly in strict alphabetical order, the job had sounded easy enough.

That wasn't always the case, as things had progressed; some files just couldn't be found anywhere in the shelving area. Melinda would double-check every piece of correspondence before placing it in the appropriate file, there for the staff to deal with in due course. The piles of found files were placed on a specific shelf in preparation for them to answer and deal with each individual correspondence methodically.

The remaining post had meant that the files were elsewhere and it was Melinda who had to go through each member of staff's paperwork on their desks and on the floor beside them in the hope of discovering a file to connect with. There was an area of shelving, there for keeping files awaiting urgent communication and newly allocated policies requiring correspondence before completion, that had eliminated a few pieces of post from her pile.

As time had gone by, Melinda had learnt to read the first few lines of each correspondence, indicating whereabouts the file itself should be; on a staff member's desk, in the urgent and newly allocated policy section or at the back of the building where all the files were kept once correspondence was completed to the staff members satisfaction. It had helped in dwindling the large pile of posts more quickly, as well as giving her an insight as to what motor insurance was all about. Melinda's job as a filing clerk was solely related to the motor industry.

At the end of the day, all finished files were heaped in a space on the floor for Melinda to place back in the shelving at the rear of the building. It was whilst doing this she had uncovered files placed incorrectly in the system. Strict alphabetical order had to be adhered to and her previous staff members had obviously not done their jobs correctly. Replacing the bogus files had unearthed outstanding posts of weeks or more, allowing the correspondence to be dealt with, finally.

She'd started a job and wanted to finish it; par for the course where Melinda was concerned. Going through each and every 'pigeonhole', the files were checked thoroughly ensuring that they were indeed in the right place. Of course, there were still some pieces of post still not linked to their appropriate files and Melinda had searched high and low before giving up before her shift had ended. She'd done her best and tomorrow was yet another day.

Temporary files would be made up until the original had been discovered but that hadn't always been enough for the staff member to be able to deal with the correspondence itself. Melinda had unearthed several files at the bottom of a pile of paperwork; something that had been put on hold and not retrieved to deal with later. This had annoyed certain staff members, who hadn't wanted to deal with the file itself but had now had no choice in the matter. Melinda was elated that she had finally linked up the outstanding post, though. Her smile had confirmed it.

Some files had been borrowed by the claims department and Melinda had put the post into the file, leaving it there for them to sort out. The typing pool, situated on the top floor of the building, was another place where files were discovered. A part of her job was to take the typed letters down to the appropriate departments once a day, enabling the staff to check and post them out the following morning. Although files shouldn't have been sent up there, some were and Melinda had ensured they were brought down, too.

Melinda's bosses were impressed with her work and within the year, she had been promoted to the motor vehicle section, along with staff members she had managed to become friendly with. Instead of finding the relevant files, she was now dealing with the correspondence placed inside them. Some cases were easy enough to deal with, whilst others had taken a lot of head-work and oceans of time.

The awkward-to-complete files had sometimes looked like she'd done nothing the whole day; Melinda was a little disappointed if she was honest. Telephone call after telephone call had caused concern about not completing the relevant paperwork the same day. As a result, that file had remained on her desk longer than anticipated. She'd now understood why there were piles of files on each staff member's desk. An uncompleted correspondence had held up the filing clerk's duties, as Melinda had recalled through sheer experience.

It was probably the reciting of letters to be sent to the customers that had appeared most daunting at first. Talking into a receiver that had linked itself to the typing pool was initially a nervous experience; hearing herself back before submitting the constructed correspondence though, was even more nerve-wracking. Did she really sound like that? The Bristolian accent wasn't the best, where she was concerned and at times Melinda had cringed at listening to herself.

With a rhotic accent, in which the post-vocalic r in words like car and card is still pronounced, having been lost from many other dialects of English, it was very much a west country voice rather than a sweet and gentile one held by other parts of the UK. It was something Melinda had to live with, unfortunately, and she had managed her job without too much deliberation, eventually. The experience had held her in good stead where letter-writing was concerned and reciting the words over the receiver. In future jobs, she'd had to speak over the office tannoy and was by then well used to hearing herself loud and clear. It was a definite confidence booster over the years, something she was more than grateful for. The hesitant, red-cheeked person of yesterday was well on her way to becoming an entirely different person.

There was much to learn in the insurance industry and Melinda had done just that. The motor department wasn't the only place she had worked in, after her stint as a filing clerk. Many more positions had her promoted and one area had sprung to mind; one with a huge grin on her face and many memories. Melinda's co-worker was a lovely man but sadly neither of them could agree on a final decision.

The personal accident insurance policy was a small affair, only taken out by a minority of customers. There to cover unforeseen mishaps whilst either working or on pleasure trips, it had paid out on sometimes obscure claims. Falling from a ladder was your normal activity, usually related to a working situation.

Premiums paid were based on their usual employment and regular pleasure pursuits; a gentleman who had enrolled in regular activities relating to heights of a sometimes dangerous nature would be 'loaded' with higher monthly payments in the eventuality of a claim than someone pursuing a somewhat relaxed job or non-dangerous activity. The risks had determined the cost of the policy and it was Melinda and her co-worker, Paul, who had to decide together on both the premiums payable and whether a claim should be paid out when one was put forward.

The disagreements as to whether to agree to the claim or not, had both Melinda and Paul raising their voices or nodding their heads when coming to a final decision. The staff seated behind and in front of them in the office, unknown to them, had been in stitches when voices were indeed raised, laughing quietly amongst themselves. As a working partnership, they had both got on really well otherwise and as friends they were inseparable; it was the indecisiveness between the two regarding the personal accident policies that had finally split them up.

Both were put into different departments and spoke regularly afterwards, there was never any animosity between them; merely differences of opinion on the work front. Melinda was moved back to the motor department but this time filling out the motorcycle policies, handwritten then. She also dealt with new quotations at the counter, adding another string to her bow. Confidence on a face-to-face basis had now excelled itself and Melinda had felt confident in sorting everything out, from the beginning until the end.

Thomas, her dad, had never asked how Melinda's job was going. The rent was paid monthly to him when she'd been paid, and not much more was said on the work front ladder. Melinda was happy in her job and had managed to remain there for almost five years. She had married Peter whilst working there. Maternity leave had halted the continuation at Phoenix Assurance and she'd not returned after her son was born, her choice in the matter.

Melinda would always look back on the years there with a smile. A good choice on her part and a lifesaver for her, personality-wise. The shy teenager had become lost in the insurance industry, turning into a more than confident adult, now a wife and a mother; all good in the context of things. Salaries weren't brilliant, if she was honest but the rewards along the way were head and heel above that. Melinda would never complain about her time there. The experience had probably saved her, over the years.

Chapter Sixteen

As life had always had the habit of causing havoc, things hadn't panned out as Melinda had planned after the arrival of her son. Her dream of becoming a twenty-four-hour housewife and mother had badly fallen on deaf ears. Apart from the financial position; she had no money coming in on her part and living was budgeted to the extreme and became a struggle, Melinda had also missed the physical contact with working employees. Something she'd not thought about at the time.

Her son couldn't have a conversation with her yet unless you included the grunts and attempted words that were completely nonsensical. She'd loved him dearly and laughed at the way he had tried so hard to get her to understand his needs at the time, there were days though when she had desperately needed an adult conversation.

Her sisters were both working, along with her brothers. Thomas and Amelia both worked, although Melinda's mum had only worked part-time, mornings during the week. Peter worked full-time hours, arriving home at approximately five-thirty in the evening on weekdays. He'd not worked weekends, thankfully a blessing.

Melinda hadn't realised how lonely life could be as a young mum. Busy as she was in taking care of him, her needs included conversation and the neighbours were elderly residents not wanting a crying or busy baby around, even for an hour or so. All completely understandable as the neighbours had included a brother and sister, neither of whom had married, and a widow who hadn't had children of her own.

It was time to look for some part-time work, she had decided and her mum had agreed to have her grandson for a few hours after her working shift. Norwich Union had come to the rescue, a vacancy requiring a four-hour day from Monday to Friday. Melinda would walk down to her mother's, a good walk pushing the baby in the pushchair, before catching the bus to her workplace. Peter would pick her up on his way home from work and they would both pick their son up from her parents' house and head for home.

Amelia had loved looking after her grandson, her second one. Melinda's brother had given her a grandson just three months prior to her own son's arrival. Having had five children in less than nine years herself, childminding wasn't new to her mother. Melinda had so revelled in having a few hours break from baby duties and had felt so much more contented in herself.

It also helped pay for the weekly grocery shopping. Prior to that, she would browse around the shops on a daily basis, pushing the baby in his pushchair to kill a few hours and return home with no more than two items of food or household requirements. Thrifty she was and had needed to be; money hadn't grown on trees!

As things had happened, six months down the line, babies had grown daily and learnt new skills. Melinda and Peter's son had been a quick learner and no exception to the rule. They'd needed eyes in the back of their head. Walking and climbing out of his cot at just ten months of age, life had become hectic. The chance of any relaxation time had disintegrated and he'd kept them on their toes, for sure.

Unfortunately for Melinda, Thomas had been used to having his evening meal on the table, or at least in the process of being cooked, when he had arrived home from work. With the baby around, Amelia had struggled to even start the evening meal. Stephen, her grandson, was busy, busy, busy. The 'terrible twos' hadn't even started and Melinda's mum was struggling to get the chores done with him around.

Her priority had to be with her husband, Melinda's dad, and reluctantly she'd informed Melinda that she wouldn't be able to look after Stephen anymore. It was understood on Amelia's part, even though she had adored looking after him. Her eyes would light up on seeing him in the pushchair as she'd finished her working shift.

Children, well young children, had brought out the best in her; she had felt needed. Thomas, on the other hand, had made it clear that having brought up five children of his own, it was his adult children's responsibility to bring up his grandchildren. Amelia would miss seeing Stephen on a daily basis, Melinda had known but hadn't argued. Nobody argued with Thomas!

It was with a sad face that her notice was given at Norwich Union, giving the reason for her untimely resignation. Without a childminder, Melinda was unable to work in any capacity; well not strictly true, evening employment once

Peter was home from work could have been found nearby. The manager had accepted her notice, reluctantly, having held her position open if she was able to find someone to look after Stephen in the near future.

Melanie, her sister, had by then given birth to a daughter, a third grandchild for Thomas and Amelia. Being a single parent soon after her entry into the world, she'd been looking for a part-time job and a childminder near her home to look after her daughter. A contact was discovered and Melinda had contacted the establishment herself asking whether Stephen could attend with them.

Aunty, as she was known to the children, took children from babies until comprehensive school years, for a fee, obviously. It was half of her take-home pay but would mean that she was at least earning something towards the living costs. They could eat a decent meal, at best. Stephen attended a trial day with the other children, there were usually ten children there at a time. Mrs Morris had an assistant to help and 'Uncle', her husband, would help out on returning home from his main job.

He'd loved it, so Norwich Union had given Melinda her job back, just six weeks after she'd handed in her notice. The downside was that they were unable to give her a permanent contract of employment but would pay her for any time she was required to work and contact her when her presence was needed again. Some work was better than none and Melinda had agreed on the terms negotiated.

She'd not needed to worry, as it happened. Her presence had lasted nine months out of twelve, every year, usually being given a break around the festive season. Three months of being able to blitz the house when not working. Stephen had still gone to 'Aunty and Uncle's' giving Melinda space to conquer jobs unable to do when there with her. A win, win situation.

Melanie's daughter had joined Stephen not long afterwards and then Stephanie, Melinda and Peter's baby daughter, had followed them when she was just four months old. A family affair it had seemed and Amelia had lost out on being there for them. She'd still seen them occasionally but not as often as she would have liked. Thomas hadn't realised how his wife had hankered to babysit her own grandchildren.

The moving of house had occurred whilst Melinda was pregnant with Stephanie. A slightly bigger place with a third bedroom, its main reason being a property with a larger garden and away from the main road. Stephen had constantly climbed the back garden wall in their first property, ending up in a pedestrian lane leading to a very busy main road. How Stephanie was ever born after Stephen's busy nature was beyond apprehension. But they managed, somehow.

The new house was nearer both Melinda's and Peter's parents (Peter's dad, his mother had passed away years earlier) and closer to 'Aunty and Uncle's', all a plus as far as they were concerned. Melinda had lived around the corner, virtually, when growing up. The area was well known to them and very familiar. Life had become a little easier than it had appeared. But sadly, not for long. Par for the course as life continues. Nothing was meant to be easy, was it?

After twenty-five years of marriage, Thomas and Amelia had separated and divorced. Stephen and Gemma, Melanie's daughter, were young children, and Melinda's daughter, Stephanie, a tiny baby. It was a sad occasion but inevitable really. They'd argued for years, big disagreements that had never been completely resolved. There was no other person involved, no affairs on either side; the relationship had just fizzled out and ran its course.

The family house and shop were sold and Thomas had rented a room in a large house locally.

Amelia was given a council property to rent with Melinda's youngest brother and sister still home. At just sixteen and seventeen years of age, they weren't ready to leave the family and start another episode of their lives. Her brother was working and earning a living, having left school at sixteen.

Her sister, Melinda was uncertain of (it was a long time ago) but shortly afterwards the patter of tiny feet had become apparent. Grandchild number four was on the way for Amelia.

Thankfully, Amelia's new home wasn't that far away; in walking distance but a short drive from their new abode. Melinda wasn't averse to walking and often did, to Amelia's home with the children in tow. Peter would pick them up after he'd finished his working shift. Still working for Norwich Union, Stephen was now in the local primary school and Stephanie was still at 'Aunty and Uncle's'. Life continued and Amelia did get to see her grandchildren a lot more often, something that she had relished.

Family was what life was all about and Amelia's life had now turned itself around. Though without her husband, now ex-husband, she'd not lost her children and had actually seen more of them than ever before. Thomas wasn't there to dictate to her so she was able to create her own rules. Children and grandchildren were her life, as it is today for Melinda. Amelia was happy and contented. The more she'd seen of her family the better she'd been for it.

Melinda's mother would always love Thomas, and did, until the day she died. Life had to go on though. She made a new life for herself amidst the darkness that had engulfed the last few years of their marriage. After living through her childhood, not a good one, losing her mother so young; Amelia's body and mind had become strong and over the years she'd coped with more than most of us could ever envisage. She was made of strong stuff, was Amelia.

Melinda's youngest sister had moved out but not until her daughter was born and the baby's dad had found a place for them to live together. Her youngest brother remained in the family home for a fair few years afterwards, until forming relationships with various female ladies, some he had set up home with before realising that things hadn't worked out.

Amelia's home became the hub of family life and she'd seldom refused to have any of her grandchildren. She was there for her own children to either work or enjoy a night out without them by their sides. A three-bedroom house it was, a small one at that but somehow she'd managed to accommodate them for a sleepover or two.

Melinda's youngest sister had gone on to have five children very quickly, two girls and three boys. Amelia was often left looking after them all and had never complained, ever. With less than nine months between the two youngest boys, it wasn't an easy feat but she'd managed, somehow. She'd felt useful towards the family and her commitment was second to none. Just the thought of caring for five youngsters today had Melinda becoming very anxious, knowing how difficult it must have been.

Thomas had made several visits to Melinda and Peter's home and he was always made to feel comfortable. Her philosophy had been one of not wanting to lose either parent and seeing him on occasion was better than not at all. At twenty-five years of age (when they'd divorced), Melinda had so found it strange for her parents to be no longer together, despite the heated disagreements over the years. They'd stuck it out for such a long time and made it work, sort of. It was a drastic change for Melinda and her siblings and even more difficult as the years progressed.

As Melinda's children had gotten older and Thomas had found a new lady in his life, visits to his new home were made, as a matter of course. Why should Stephen and Stephanie miss out on seeing their granddad? Thomas had a new family now, five stepchildren, three of whom were still living at home. She'd tried to include them in her life, as best she could.

Children will be children as we all know. Both Stephen and Stephanie were told not to let 'nanny' know that they'd gone to visit their granddad and they hadn't uttered a word to her. Just mentioning Thomas's name would have rendered an unhappy Amelia. Better for her, that she'd not known at all. Despite everything, Amelia still loved Thomas but you couldn't turn the clock back, sadly.

Chapter Seventeen

Melinda and Peter's annual holiday usually included Amelia, after Thomas had left. Somehow, they'd both wanted to include her and spoil her. Peter had treated her similarly to his own mother, one he had adored until her death from cancer just six weeks after their marriage. He was allowed to criticise her, shout at her and more than once had told her to 'get on her broomstick and fly away'. She had allowed him to do it but if Melinda or her siblings had repeated the same words to her they would have been landed with a 'clipped ear' for their cheek. Peter could wrap her around his little finger and did. With that said, Amelia had revelled in the attention and loved her holidays as a family. A helping hand as well as a companion, the annual holiday was always looked forward to. Stephanie was just six months old when they had spent a week's break at a Pontins holiday park in Brixham, Devon. A camp set high above the waters of a beautiful town, so loved by Melinda, even today. The clubhouse was where Amelia had stood up on stage and revealed her favourite celebrity of all time and she was told to run to the gentleman at the end of the stage calling out his name. She had, to Melinda and Peter's amazement; Des O'Connor being her heart-throb of the era.

Melinda's mum was coming out of her shell!

As years progressed, a lot of years, Melinda and Peter had often booked breaks away to Brixham and never tired of staying there. It's there on Melinda's bucket list to visit in the future, on her own; the memories of family holidays in Brixham would never fade and hadn't needed to. The art gallery, still there, was a frequent calling and three landscapes painted by local artists were purchased over the years.

Austria was the first place abroad that they'd taken Amelia to. A week's coach travel through France and Belgium before reaching their destination. Coincidence or not, they had stopped in France overnight where a hotel fire had engulfed the area. The name of the hotel was Bristol Hotel, the city they had lived in. Thankfully, nobody was hurt in the fire albeit a lot of damage to the building itself.

Austria in August was stunning; scrupulously clean, you could eat your food from the pavement. The hotel was of a high standard, the food something of a mish-mash of English and Austrian cuisine. Fish soup was served one night with the fish's eyes staring up at you through the clear colourless liquid. Not for the faint-hearted; neither of them had eaten that evening. Nobody starved though and the experience was second to none, a true learning curve.

The coach full of holidaymakers had all felt sorry for her one afternoon. Their free day from excursions, educating them on the historic facts and places around them was spent in the local park.

Amelia had been sunning herself on the grass whilst the children were playing in the playground.

Peter was keeping an eagle eye on them. Melinda and Peter had protected themselves from the hot sun above with suntan lotion. Amelia had declined; a lady of dark pigment during the summer months had never burnt, her words, and one she would eat up some few hours later.

As they'd returned to the hotel for their evening meal, her legs had turned a brighter shade of red, a deep crimson red. It had looked so sore. Within hours, Amelia's attempt to dress for dinner was excruciatingly painful, her face showing it. Anything touching the 'lobster' limbs had caused immense pain and she had really struggled. Mother is always right, isn't she? Not when they're wrong! We all live and learn and learn she had that afternoon, for sure.

It was in Spain, with Peter's dad and his siblings, that Amelia was mistaken for a native. Her complexion and skin tone were akin to the residents there and some had tried to communicate with her, in Spanish; Amelia hadn't understood a word they had said. She had, in all honesty, fitted into the area. A petite lady of older years, of slight build and bronzed in all the right places. The Spanish and the Greeks had looked after their elderly relatives, treating them with kid gloves; the matriarch of the family, so precious. The older descendants were well looked after and looked up to.

It was in Greece, a place visited often, with and without Amelia, that the traffic would stop to let her cross the road. Merely holding up her walking stick to them, they had obediently shut down their engines for her before continuing their journey. Peter had laughed at her as she'd stopped the flow of traffic, muttering something sarcastic under his breath and allowing him to repeat it out aloud.

Melinda's body would have received a tap from the stick if she had uttered something similar.

Amelia's son-in-law was a sure favourite in her eyes. The only son-in-law, at that.

The waiters had received constant criticism where food was concerned. A Greek salad was devoid of lettuce, a normal custom there but Melinda's mum had insisted on a lettuce leaf to accompany the sliced cucumbers, tomatoes, green bell peppers, red onion, olives and feta cheese. Only the matriarch of the family would have been allowed the privilege. Amelia's facial smirk was childlike, she could play them to her advantage and had relished in the thought. At times, she'd had the devil inside her. Salad wasn't salad without a lettuce leaf! Who was to argue?

"I only want five chips," she'd told one waiter and he had given her a smaller portion than usual. Counting the fried potatoes, there were more than five on her plate and as a consequence, he was reprimanded. Peter and Melinda had laughed aloud, Amelia was incorrigible.

"I only want one piece of toast with scrambled egg on," she had said to the same waiter the following morning. "I can't eat two slices." This time he hadn't obliged. The price had befitted two slices with scrambled egg on and he'd been unable to alter the price to suit. A scornful look had adorned her face, momentarily. Stubborn, Amelia was but a truly memorable character, one sorely missed today. Melinda, for one, had struggled without her mother, for many years.

A childlike Amelia had revelled in the hot sunshine in Greece and she had made herself comfortable on the lounger on the beach, her skin getting darker and darker by the minute; she was loving every minute of it. Stephen had made her dream come true there, catching hold of her arms and taking her carefully into the sea to allow the waves to wrap themselves around her slight body, holding her balance intact.

It may have been Stephen's wedding break but he had made time for his grandmother and given her the thrill she had wanted back then. For Amelia, waves were hypnotic to her, even when so much younger; the times she'd jumped into the water to catch them and emerged looking similar to a drowned rat had occurred frequently when on holiday. She couldn't help herself. Occasions to recall and smile about now. Her face had lit up afterwards, the exhilaration complete.

She could scowl, too. Not a pretty sight for Melinda and her siblings. Were they in for a telling-off? More often than not, yes. Stubbornness was something inherited and passed on throughout the family and generations. Melinda would own up to being a tad stubborn, at times. Peter would walk away from Amelia (and Melinda) when the scowl had emerged. It had usually done the trick.

However, Melinda's mum's escapades abroad had nearly never happened at all. Without a passport to travel, her initial attempt had almost failed, miserably. In obtaining a birth certificate to send with the passport application, her letter to the Wareham library had not found her birth in their records. She had existed, there were five children of hers to clarify it. The proof was there. Melinda had spoken to the library on the telephone, bemused. On rechecking Amelia's letter, the receptionist had said that she'd stated her birthplace as Poole rather than Wareham, both areas tracked from the library itself, individually. The Poole inventory showed no sign of Melinda's mum but Wareham's register had her there, clearly. Phew! Amelia's heart had almost stopped with the shock. Long Lost Family had suddenly filled her head. Why had she made that mistake? It was her youngest sister who had been born in Poole Hospital!

The birth certificate would be in the post the following day, Melinda was told. Several days later, Amelia had informed her of receiving the elusive certificate and her actual age. She was a year older than she had thought she had been all along! Was there any hope for Melinda and her siblings? Apart from getting married for the first time, she'd never had any reason to check on her birth certificate and the years had rolled by. Amelia could be excused, this time!

The hiccup had caused a lot of laughter over the years for one reason or another. She had, in all fairness, taken it in good stead. How can anyone forget how old they are, or at least their date of birth? Amelia obviously had and could have missed out on a whole year's state pension. She did continue working after her sixtieth birthday, admittedly; monies owed to her would have been lost to her, though.

With her passport obtained, she did travel, with and without Melinda and Peter; all good in the context of things. She'd deserved it and had worked hard over the years. The UK and areas she'd lived as a child, were of particular interest as the years had passed. Melinda had wanted to know all about her childhood and the residential areas she'd lived in.

Her stories of the past had sent Melinda and Peter to find her and her parents' living regions since Amelia's death. Intriguing, interesting and inquisitive of her living years; the findings of her existence were something to reveal about. Stubborn even then, the tales of her childhood were a story to behold. Melinda and her siblings had inherited a lot of her characteristics, definitely. Finding Amelia's father's birthplace, sadly the local workhouse, now turned into luxury apartments but still there to imagine in its heyday, was indeed inspirational. The house he had lived in as a child with his grandparents, was something that neither Melinda or her younger sister had expected or were prepared for. Taking their mother there, just three weeks before her death had been precious to her. An area of Warwickshire with huge expanses of countryside and a small hamlet of houses affording the glorious views every single day living. He was indeed spoilt. The chocolate box village nearby was where ancestors of Harry's (Amelia's father) were buried in the churchyard. How did Melinda and her family end up in Bristol? A large city without the prettiness that Stratford-upon-Avon and its surroundings had afforded. Melinda, for one, was so envious of her grandfather's roots, his birth roots anyway.

Amelia had passed away knowing where her father had come from, something that had taken a lot of delving into to discover over the years. He'd not spoken about his past that much. Her smile had shown complete elation and she had wanted to revisit the area, something that was sadly denied her. Not by choice, Melinda would have willingly taken her there again.

As a child, Amelia hadn't always conformed to her parents' or grandparents' rules, especially where her step-grandmother was concerned. She so disliked her but was forced to live with her after her own mother's death. A young girl treated as a slave in the house, it had been no wonder. She'd adored her grandfather, her mother's father, but he had passed away whilst she was in his care.

Amelia's stories of hating her boots purchased by her step-grandmother, so much so that she'd trodden into the mud in the cow shed where she had tied the cows up in preparation for milking, before heading off to school in the morning. Hiding the repulsive boots behind the sofa in the hallway, a place where they wouldn't have been found, Amelia had never worn them again. Melinda could re-enact the moment now, with Amelia's devious grin a focal point.

Sent to work in service at fourteen years of age in the local vicarage and living in, Amelia was somewhat relieved. She'd loved it there and was treated with respect by the widowed lady of the vicarage and her two daughters, one of them a nun. Dorchester itself was again a countryside haven and Melinda had felt humbled that her own mother had lived there for part of her life. Norton-St-Philip, Lullington, Dorchester, Wareham and various areas around Dorset, Amelia's childhood was spent in idyllic locations. Whether she'd realised it or not at the time, Melinda had envied the beautiful areas her mother had frequented. Bristol was where she'd met Thomas, next-door neighbours in fact. Things had happened for a reason and Melinda and her siblings were a consequence of that, a good consequence. Well, most of the time, that was.

Memories are a strange thing; the mind would think about certain events at the most inappropriate times. Melinda's thoughts now were about Peter and Amelia, the good times rather than the bad episodes. There were plenty of those, for sure. Life had a habit of upsetting the apple cart, so to speak. Being tested, Melinda would have called it.

Photographs of life gone by, places lived in and living as it was in Amelia's childhood and going way back. All was not so bad, hard work admittedly but families were close, so much closer than today. Money, at times, has a habit of clouding what is important. Family first, always; that was Melinda's philosophy, rightly or wrongly and nothing could change her mind on that score.

Chapter Eighteen

Moving to South Wales, Melinda had found part-time work in the local public house. Initially, it was kitchen duties but had then included waitressing on a weekday evening and sometimes on a weekend. Peter was home with the children, so it had suited them both. Peter had found work in the building trade eventually; it had taken a few months to secure a position but the house purchased had needed a lot of work done on it so he wasn't twiddling his thumbs at all. There was plenty to do. After working for over twenty years in a foundry, he'd wanted outdoor work; not cooped up inside a factory building all day long.

Whilst working in the local public house a part-time vacancy had arisen just four miles away, in insurance. Covering staff holidays and sickness days, she had managed to juggle both jobs for a long time. Christmas parties had worn her out along with the insurance work, at times her head hadn't registered where she was. She would wake up from sleep and walk into the wardrobe, thinking that she was still at work. Giving up the waitressing, Melinda had concentrated on the day job.

With Stephen now in comprehensive school and Stephanie able to walk home from school with friends and their parents, Stephen wasn't long behind her and Peter home from work shortly afterwards. Childminding was at a minimum and Melinda wasn't working all the time, all good there. They were good children, she would have to admit.

Life seemed to sail along at a steady pace, normal living as they say. Nothing dramatic occurred and no emergencies to deal with of any sort, well nothing major anyway. No catastrophes or anything sinister to start the pulses racing or cause any havoc. No complaints whatsoever. Living as it should be, calming and simple; days plodding along nicely.

Wales was lived at a much slower pace at first, more of a laid-back approach rather than the hustle and bustle of a busy city; Bristol's constant traffic, running here and there non-stop with no time to breathe was mind-blowing at times. Sadly, that had all changed as the children had grown. Wanting lifts here and there, picking one or the other up from college etc. Things became more erratic, a culture shock and life had become busy yet again.

Peter's dad had died not long after moving to South Wales and although he was promised a stay at theirs, he had passed away in hospital before getting there. Melinda could still hear his words in the hospital. "I'm not going to get to spend time at yours, am I?" All the reassurance in the world hadn't changed the outcome. He never did make it, more is the pity. "Can you watch television in Wales?" He'd asked when they were moving from Bristol to South Wales. Melinda still smiled at the question asked, with him thinking that they were moving to some third-world country.

Melinda's nan was born in South Wales, the Rhondda Valley to be exact, so the Welsh accent wasn't new to her. She had loved her nan dearly and missed her dreadfully. With

Melinda's youngest brother moving to the Rhondda Valley, his wife had taken her to her birthplace in Llwnypia, the house she'd lived with her first husband and the house her grandfather had lived with his first wife. One street away from each other, they'd both met after the passing of their first spouses.

Photographs taken of the residences had brought Melinda's grandparents back to life and even though she was only eight years old when her granddad had passed away, she could still see his kind face looking up at her from the bed in the living room where he had died. Born in Bristol, he had moved to the Rhondda Valley for work where he'd met his first wife. Settled there for years, Nan and Granddad had moved back to Bristol, where they had remained until their deaths.

Life had somehow completed a circle. Two of their grandchildren had relocated to South Wales, namely Melinda and Colin. No complaints whatsoever; ups and downs were normal activity on the life score. Melinda's children were now fluent in the Welsh language, both married now. Stephen is married to a Welsh-born lady and Stephanie to an English 'evacuee' who had studied at Swansea University and remained there in the neighbourhood.

All the grandsons are Welsh by birth and Melinda couldn't be more proud. Some speak the Welsh language and others still learning. Her nan's words still echoed in Melinda's ears and always would. "Come by yer, Bach," she would say often, being just one of the country's expressions that had continued until her death at ninety-six years of age. Melinda, for one, was more than happy to have Welsh blood flowing throughout her body; slightly diluted admittedly but still there all the same.

Several other jobs had Melinda trying her hand at. Yet another insurance position had evolved, this time in a brokerage rather than a company itself. Reception work had followed before really branching out and heading in a completely different direction altogether. Selling ceramic tiles and wood flooring was a new one for her and she'd been uncertain that she would succeed in the post, once started.

With help from staff members, Melinda had surprised herself. Always being good at colour coordination, she could envisage a customer's bathroom or kitchen with their description and sometimes rough drawings and head them in the right direction. Compliments of their results were, on occasion, related back to her with a prominent thumbs up.

Initially, working out the amount of tiles or wood flooring required, along with the adhesive, grout, spacers etc., wasn't always easy. Some customers were 'old school' people who only worked in feet and inches; the children of pounds, shillings and pence, Melinda's era and earlier. Metres, the system used today was sometimes mixed with yards, causing even more headaches and reworking out of measurements. Melinda had managed it eventually and with very few tiles or packs of wood flooring returned for a refund; surplus to requirements, it had seemed, her estimated purchase was pretty good.

Assistant manager status was given to her on her next job, again in ceramic tiles and wood flooring. Dealing with the paperwork side of things, ordering products and returns, along with the manual lifting of the products and dealing with deliveries; Melinda had surprisingly revelled in the job until her health had begun to deteriorate due to all the heavy lifting entailed.

Just five feet and one inch tall, the job had taken its toll on her back and she'd recalled customers warning her of health issues to come due to the workload itself. At the time she'd dismissed it as nonsense but all had become a reality, at the end. Peter's job in the building trade had realised the same and near the end of his years in work, the pressures on his body had shown, as well as being felt.

How Melinda had managed to secure a position employed by a bookmaker, she'd not known. Not really sport-orientated at all, an interview was passed with flying colours. The work itself, she'd realised before applying for the job, was going to be stressful head-wise; the crowning glory being a pretty much sit-down job.

It was yet another culture shock for Melinda. Having to work out the odds of winning bets, capture the bets themselves and equip oneself with two noisy fruit machines, she'd surprised herself with how quickly she'd learnt the ropes. The meeting up of customers wanting to place small, medium and large bets on various different sports was an eye-opener, if she was honest with herself. How much did they want to bet on one horse race? She would never have parted with so much money herself but it wasn't her money, was it?

The Grand National horse race was the pinnacle of all races. Historically, the first race was run in 1839 and is a handicap steeplechase over an official distance of about four miles and two and a half furlongs. Horses jump over thirty fences over two laps, with the fences being of a huge height in places.

The race itself is run at Aintree Racecourse and the horses requirements include being seven years old and up. The betting shop itself, on that one day of the year, became a fairground; people came out of the woodwork to place a bet on the iconic race. Ones who rarely bet on anything but traditionally had picked out a name from a hat, placing a small deposit on a horse being shown to run in the event, one of many.

A sometimes dangerous occasion, if Melinda was entirely true to herself. Horses were injured on falling, some having to be put down because of it. Watching the race itself was a heart wrenching experience at the best of times. Melinda would shout to the television screen 'Please get up', after a horse had fallen. She did not want the animal to lose its life. Regardless, the race was a day of the year that the bookmakers were and still are reliant on.

From opening that morning until the start of the race, the shop would be manic. Queue after queue of customers placing bets, asking questions and wanting advice on the betting procedure. There was no time to breathe, much less afford a break for a cuppa or a sandwich. The day hadn't stopped, literally.

As soon as the race was over, the crowds would re-emerge, to collect their winnings. The show had to go on, so to speak. It was a privilege to honour customers with their winnings, though really the bookmakers hadn't wanted the favourites to win or be placed in the final four. Losers had added to the company's pot and there were an awful lot of losers in the crowd of punters. It was anyone's race, The Grand National; a loose horse hitting the favourite would often jolt the rider and result in him becoming dismounted.

The hype of the race was so much so, that families would congregate around their television sets with their eyes glued to the horses jumping over the fences, willing their choices on to finish the race. Melinda had recalled Thomas, her dad, placing an old decimal shilling each on a horse for her, her siblings and a larger amount for him and Amelia. Their nan had been a regular there too, though her heart was always into the wrestling, she'd loved watching it.

Eight years, she'd remained in the bookmakers. A surprise for Thomas, who hadn't really agreed with her new employment status; he'd not liked her working in insurance either, so what was new there? Melinda's working experience was coming to an end, sadly. She'd not realised it but through no fault of her own, the boots had needed hanging up, for good.

At fifty-four years of age, Melinda's body had begun to retaliate. A hard-working wife, mother and grandmother, she'd not stopped for breath for years. From taking her eldest grandson to the nursery, continuing on to work and putting a twelve-hour shift in, she'd called into the twenty-four-hour supermarket and bought groceries for the next few days.

Peter would have already prepared himself a meal and would be sound asleep on the comfy chair when she had returned home that evening. A meal equating to cheese on toast or a sandwich would suffice, along with a cup of much-needed tea. Work days were just that, there was no chance of relaxing, none at all.

On days off, Melinda would look after her grandson and try to get some much-needed housework done. All wasn't doable and weekends were workdays where Melinda was concerned. The bookmakers didn't close on a weekend. Days off were never the same days, so the organisation didn't exist. Plodding on, more like and keeping going; manual lifting was now null and void but the bookmaker's work was stressful, more stressful than she'd ever expected.

Feeling unwell for no particular reason had been the start of things to come. Blowing hot and cold, tired and lethargic; her body had indicated that something was not quite right. Melinda had persevered, shrugging her symptoms off as being on the go all the time, with no time to breathe and totally relax. That had to be the reason, hadn't it? She wasn't getting any younger!

A standard appointment, one due to her age, had indicated otherwise. Appointments had now become fast and furious before a diagnosis was eventually issued. Melinda, for one, hadn't expected the consultant's reason for the sudden lethargic reaction her body was portraying. It had suddenly hit home a few days later though and she knew that her working days were now well and truly numbered.

Chapter Nineteen

As a teenager growing up, Melinda's ideas of what she had and hadn't wanted were crystal clear. During her school days at St George's Grammar School, the jobs in her head didn't include factory work. Nothing specific had lit up for her reasoning apart from working alongside a conveyor belt for eight hours a day, five days a week. That had sounded monotonous, repetitive and boring. There was a working sausage factory in Totterdown years ago. A place where workers had added the prepared sausage meat to their skins, replicating today's popular product. Sausages were the working man's equivalent to a succulent steak during the week; sausage and mashed potato being very popular as an evening meal for the whole family, even now.

Melinda had, on occasion, watched the workers walking out of the factory building looking tired and forlorn, after a working day's shift. Stinking of sausage meat and the skins, generally made from the submucosa of the intestines of meat animals (beef, sheep and pigs), she'd known that that wasn't her calling for the future. Regardless of the salary, she'd not wanted to go down that route.

University and extra studying weren't on the cards either. Being a quiet, naive person devoid of too much confidence,

Melinda had contented herself with mediocre jobs that had required a little brainwork; nothing too complicated or alarming. Working a simple office procedure as tidily and correctly as possible had ticked all the boxes for her. Even then, she had made mistakes, no one was infallible.

She had no illusions of becoming a brain surgeon, or anything anywhere near equivalent; Melinda had left that to her youngest sister, seven years her junior, who was the more intelligent of her siblings; not that any of them were less than normal, in the education criteria, that was. Each and every one of them was capable of holding down a secure job position in the future and had. Melinda's sister, the youngest of the two, was super intelligent at primary school. A photographic memory from an early age, she had radiated confidence and was always the bright star, prominently in front where being noticed was concerned. A pretty child and the tallest of all the siblings, she was destined to go far.

Melinda had happily remained in the background, never wanting to be the centre of attention or to become the boss of any business. A wallflower, at best, was where she had remained throughout her working life. Being a spokesperson for any working position was never something Melinda could have coped with or would have wanted to be a part of. Standing in front of an audience would have probably been her worst nightmare, not that she'd ever tried it.

A salary enough to manage from leaving school at fifteen years of age had continued throughout her working life. Never destined to be rich, she was content, if she was being completely honest. A savings account had steadily increased, always thrifty from an early age she had smelled out the bargain rack in the shops, never complaining about being unable to afford the higher priced alternatives.

Holidays were never extravagant, well, not in the beginning anyway. As the years had passed, with Stephen and Stephanie all grown up and living their own lives, she had splashed out a little on bucket list vacations for both Peter and herself. Even then, Melinda had mulled over the cost carefully before booking them up, throwing caution to the wind before questioning whether she'd done the right thing.

Today, she'd realised that she had, having lost her husband and treasured their memories together. The expense had been well worth it, knowing that the experience could never be repeated. That balcony outside their rooms on the cruise liner heading for Alaska had cost a lot of added pennies to the holiday but it was certainly worth it. The jacuzzi bath in the ensuite bathroom was something else, too. Luxury at its best.

The views had well outweighed the extra cost, something that will never be deleted from Melinda's mind; well, hopefully not! You only live once. she'd reminded herself. A week's luxury, touching shoulders with the upper class was something relished when there and the daily jacuzzi bath had helped her body to relax, totally. There were no regrets, none at all.

Melinda had sometimes questioned herself, telling her brain off and even thinking badly of her earlier choices in life. Could she have gone further down the road and improved on her past experiences? Her head had nodded, negatively. No, no, Melinda had managed to the best of her capabilities. She was never destined to outshine others in her path. Her place had been mapped out for her, for sure.

Where she is now, is where she was meant to be, like it or not. Melinda was Melinda!

Finances and work capabilities aside, Melinda's only other wish, after finishing school that was, was to own her own house. Not looking for a mansion or a villa overlooking the ocean (though that would have been nice), her prime concern was to have a property in her name at some point in her life. She wasn't in any hurry and was prepared to accept however long it had taken to reach her goal. *Rome wasn't built in a day* or even two days!

Renting, whether by private rental or through the local council, to Melinda was a waste of money. Paying a mortgage was gradually purchasing a property; the number of years before completion had been neither here nor there. Slowly and surely was better than not at all. Melinda's fear was of growing older and unable to afford to rent anywhere to live.

Her fear had been justified. Since losing Peter, she would never be able to pay the monthly rental of today. Her state pension wouldn't have covered it. Owning the house they had both worked so hard for had finally earned its own rewards. A roof over her head until life had pushed her in other directions; a nursing home or joining Peter was in her mind.

With the cost of living causing near poverty to many families today, Melinda was managing, just about. Not averse to cutting back, she'd known that the roof over her head couldn't be taken from her. Peace of mind, she'd called it and that was exactly what it was. Her concerns were halted, even though some luxuries were forfeited along the way.

The status of living in a council house hadn't been a reason for her early decision. A lot of the houses owned by the council were far superior to private properties around about. More space to bring a family up in and an easier lifestyle, in the short term; further down the line of life rent would still be required paying.

Melinda was a worrier and the future had concerned her. Whether her life would be a short or long one, being able to afford basic necessities was constantly on her mind. Never expecting a bank account filled with a huge rainy day fund, being able to pay the incoming bills was paramount in her head.

Humiliation, big time, if needing to ask for help from family members or elsewhere was concerned. Melinda was a proud person and would sooner starve than ask. What she couldn't afford she couldn't have, as simple as that. Putting an extra layer of clothing on rather than increasing the temperature on the central heating control wasn't that difficult and had served its purpose. This had held strong in needing support for anything, not necessarily money-orientated. For any tasks required, Melinda would try her best to do herself, before asking for help elsewhere. With Peter always being the man about the house, any repairs or general day-to-day jobs were always his domain. Having to learn herself, some things were definitely not among her capabilities.

Changing a lightbulb was okay, as long as she'd been careful about climbing up and down the stepladder. One day, she would miss her footing, she knew, falling badly and causing injury to herself. Until then though, Melinda would plod on in her own way. The time would come when she couldn't climb the stepladder at all, that was a worry.

Stephen had helped on occasion and Melinda was so grateful. Replacing a dimmer switch, putting up a watercolour painting and obtaining a loft ladder were just a few things recalled. Her neighbour had rehung a curtain pole when one of Melinda's grandsons had accidentally pulled it down. It had obviously been loose in the first place, something that had happened over years of constant use.

Checking on the small car Melinda owned was something that Stephen had kept an eye on for her. Small things that she was so appreciative of. Peter was so missed for many reasons, keeping things up together being just one of them. In all fairness, her son-in-law had helped too, since Peter had passed away. Special people helped Melinda to cope alone.

Owning her property, Melinda's wish, it had been immaterial whether she'd married Peter, or anyone else for that matter. She would have achieved it on her own, somehow and eventually. Harder, it would have been but when determined Melinda had usually managed to realise her future hopes, ones that were realistic anyway. Somewhere, during her lifetime, the expectation, the dream, would have been granted. A small one-bedroomed apartment it probably would have been but hers, nevertheless.

Melinda's head had never perceived anything remotely associated with the rich and the famous. Her confidence and self-esteem were way too low for that. Speaking out was something she had taken from others often rather than done herself. Curling up into a little ball or climbing back into her shell, rhetorically speaking, her shyness had been brought to the surface as a child. Things had changed slightly as she'd aged and brought up two children of her own. Tempers flared on several occasions and at times, Melinda's voice was heard rather loudly. Stubbornness had run in the family and she'd not been excluded there, for certain. An angry Amelia was indeed a frightening one!

She had usually lost the fight, so to speak and had crumbled quietly in a corner. Admitting defeat, Melinda would go along with the crowd's decision, not venturing further with her own opinions, regardless of the importance in her head. A coward, she would probably be called today but anything for a peaceful life. Young or old, male or female, Melinda had accepted her lot after burying her head in the sand for a little while.

Her relationship with Peter was different and any decisions, although discussed beforehand, had Melinda winning and coming up trumps. A placid person, there to please, Peter rarely denied anything where his wife and family were concerned. After a few huffs and puffs initially, he'd gone along with the crowd and not complained aloud.

She'd been lucky in marrying Peter, Melinda had known; not often had he refused anything affordable or uttered the word 'No'. She'd been very spoilt on that score, she'd known. Peter could never be replaced and she did not want to replace him. Melinda's life was mapped out from now on, centred around her children and grandchildren. They were more important now, more so than ever.

Amelia, Melinda's mum, had followed the same path at the end. After remarrying years after getting divorced from Thomas, the relationship failed after a few short years, leaving her on her own yet again. Becoming an independent person after twenty-five years of marriage to Melinda's dad, Thomas, she'd struggled to include another person permanently in her world twenty-four hours a day; regardless of the fact that he had wanted to spoil her and often did.

Melinda, nearly four years down the line, would probably relate exactly the same way as her own mum had. Going backwards after living alone would be far more demanding than she was now used to or prepared for. The grandchildren couldn't be included there; the infectious little beings could wrap themselves around Melinda's little finger and did. There was nothing she wouldn't do for them or go the extra mile for. The babies of today, destined to be the adults of the future.

Grandma was equally as important to them and vice versa.

Chapter Twenty

Melinda's life had come a long way. Whether she'd a few years left or a lot longer, wasn't known to her. She'd not wanted to know and wasn't psychic, thankfully. The remaining years would pass by quicker than expected, as is life; judging by the weeks turned into months and then into years, time couldn't be stopped, ever. Time was immaterial as long as it was used well. Had Melinda managed her years on a good note?

To the best of her capabilities, she'd plodded on. Times had been good, bad and indifferent over the years. Episodes of pure happiness and hysteria, par for the course, if she was honest. Future plans had not been realised, due to illnesses and eventually death. Plans and bucket lists were drawn up over the years but hadn't materialised, well not all of them.

Melinda's idea of living a full life from an early age included a husband, children and grandchildren. She couldn't complain there, all had come to fruition. Five grandsons and a sixth grandchild yet to make an appearance, both Peter and Melinda had been blessed, well and truly. The grandchildren were indeed idolised, spoilt and a reason to continue living. Baby people taking over the world with their unique personalities. So adorable, who could ever harm them?

Two cats had been treated equally, similar to spoilt children. Melinda had cried bucket loads when putting her twenty-year-old moggy to sleep, having contracted cancer in her mouth. She still missed her, settled on her lap and digging her claws into her clothing, purring with contentment. Refusing to have any more animals because of the love and fear of losing them, a pet-free house it had become and will remain so. There were enough tears flowing as things were today, Melinda hadn't wanted to add any more to the equation.

Watching a movie on the television with one of her grandsons, one about a missing dog, had Melinda in tears with him questioning her reason for crying.

"It was a good ending, Grandma," he'd said. It was, the dog had been found and lived a happy life with its owners.

Melinda couldn't answer him. The following week he'd asked to re-watch the movie and the tears were flowing yet again. She'd loved pets but had stuck to her decision. No more pets, ever. Her heart wouldn't take any more sadness and allow her to shed any more tears. Seeing other people's pets around and patting their heads would have to suffice.

Children and animals were the pinnacle of what life had represented. Without them, things would be so dull. Melinda's youngest grandson, at just fifteen months old, was a live wire and getting into everything. He had just learnt how to press the button on the washing machine and how to open the oven door and climb into it, much to his mother's annoyance. She'd no washing to do and thankfully the oven wasn't on.

Busy, busy, busy he was and had put a smile on everyone's faces. A joy to watch dancing to music and a determined child when wanting to click the safety clasp on his highchair (and pushchair) together. Melinda had suddenly remembered the eldest boy, now sixteen years of age, refusing her help in securing his seat belt in her car when taking him to school in the morning.

"I can do it," he would say and wouldn't give in until he had managed it.

His youngest brother was following in his footsteps, for sure. A curiosity for fixing things together, whether it was clasps or placing pegs into holes; the concentration on his little face was a serious affair. He was going to succeed in life, somehow Melinda could tell. Boys will be boys. Melinda's grandsons were infectious from birth; watching them grow was a true privilege.

The middle boy, when less than two years old had known where the food cupboard was in Melinda's kitchen. He would be seen sitting inside the cupboard eating a biscuit, having thrown all of the cans of food out onto the floor in front of him. The kitchen had been updated since then, the last room to be done before Peter's passing. The pantry shelves weren't accessible to the 'little one' at the moment; children grow quickly so it was only a matter of time!

The baby's 'noodles' in his hair were getting tighter and tighter as he'd progressed in months. The only one to have curls galore, so cute and the middle boy's reference to his brother's hair as 'noodles' was laughable, so funny.

"They look like noodles," he'd said. He was right, the comparison was similar.

Who could be sad with the grandchildren around, not Melinda? They had lifted her moods, raised her spirits and made her feel important, whether she was or not. Precious little beings they were (well two of them, the eldest being five feet nine inches in height). Life would be so lonely without them.

Melinda had been so grateful for their existence, even more so now that Peter wasn't around. Just imagining herself completely on her own, isolated from people of all descriptions; it wasn't worth contemplating. Melinda would have hated it. Heaven may have taken Peter from her but the family were still there. Whether she was there for them or the other way around hadn't mattered. Melinda was still a part of their world for the foreseeable future and she'd thanked her lucky stars as she'd looked up to the sky. Knowing that loneliness would have killed her well before her time, someone up there was indeed looking after her. Peter would have worked his magic to ensure that family life had continued, Melinda had been certain.

Standing at the bottom of the 99 steps, now a sixty-seven-year-old widow, Melinda had looked around her. The park was still there, that hadn't changed at all. The main road still took cars from Totterdown to Bedminster, travelling under the railway bridge; a bridge still there for the regular train journeys departing from Temple Meads Station.

Everything else around had completely changed, sadly. Gone were the terraced houses on both sides of the road, along with the small public houses where locals had frequented for the odd pint or two after a hard day's work; earning pennies to feed their large families. Gone were the people, the community as it was.

Gone was the small rank of shops that had welcomed trade from neighbours on a daily basis and gone was Melinda's childhood home; still there but used for a different purpose entirely. Gone were the older people of her childhood, all passed away and now residing with God in heaven. New faces walked the steps and the road. Strangers in her childhood neighbourhood, so young and innocent. Beginning their lives in a place that was once so special to Melinda.

Memories of her growing up, playing in the park, walking to work after leaving school. They were vivid in her mind, as was climbing the 99 steps to deliver the Sunday newspapers to residents waiting to catch up on the news of the day, the week passed and the activities of the imminent future. Melinda had been the child that had given them that information, posting the newspapers through their letterboxes every Sunday morning.

Gone was her childhood friend, Glyn and a previous boyfriend, both passing away far too young from cancer, the disease that Melinda had survived but Peter hadn't. A cruel disease that had cut short so many lives, Peter's mother included. She had passed away just six short weeks after Melinda and Peter's wedding day, holding on to be there to see them both married.

Gone was Amelia, her mum, now there up above, with her passed family. She was missed so much, more than words could ever describe. A voice at the end of the telephone, a place to visit and stay over, keeping her company as she'd aged. A person to remember for the right and wrong reasons throughout her eighty-two years of life; nobody was perfect, not even Melinda's mum. Gone was the primary school she'd attended and the local shops opposite it. All destroyed and new buildings now stood pride of place, all there for other purposes. Houses becoming flats, purpose built for the young of today; equipped with all the mod cons not recognised when

Melinda was younger. Spoilt, the people of today were, for certain. A fully equipped bathroom, central heating, and bespoke kitchens with lots of cupboard space; that was just for starters.

Melinda and her family had managed to survive in a three-storey property where the bathroom facilities were situated on the lowest level. Two flights of stairs to climb down to relieve yourself during the night. They had all managed and never complained. The plastic bucket in Thomas and Amelia's bedroom had been a source of urgency when desperately needed. That was life as it was for most people of the time. What you hadn't had, you didn't miss. A saying so, so true.

The children of today, those becoming adults of the future, well most of them anyway; some would reach heaven in their younger years, through no fault of their own. They would never know what normal living was, back in Melinda's childhood days. She'd not have changed it though, if a wish was granted.

There were good days, bad days and normal days along the way. All a learning curve for tomorrow, one would think. That wasn't always the case, not for Melinda. Sometimes, bad times had turned into terrible times; ones that had festered for years before mending. Things that she'd had to live with. Sometimes a simple apology wasn't enough, not sufficient.

Gone was Peter's brother and youngest sister and recently a much-loved cousin of his (as well as his parents, years ago). At ninety-five years of age, she'd placed flowers on Peter's grave before passing away herself shortly afterwards. Melinda's nephew had died suddenly at just thirty-one years young. His young son will never see him grow older.

People from Bristol, Melinda's birthplace, all now living it up in heaven. At times, she'd wanted to join them but had known that it wasn't her time just yet. Patience is a virtue and Melinda would hold on, even when loneliness was apparent. Whether her future years would be fruitful, Melinda wouldn't know until the time came.

Gone were the pleasure trips to Portishead and Clevedon on a weekend with the children (Stephen and Stephanie). Burnham-on-Sea held special memories, Peter had loved the OXO machines on the pier, a young lad had enlightened him on how to win rather than lose his money.

Not enough to buy a house but sufficient to enable a free day out. All good in the context of things.

Money hadn't grown on trees then and still doesn't now. That would be magical!

Since moving to South Wales, it was Pembrokeshire that had held special memories for Melinda; Fishguard being a particular favourite for both Peter and his wife. Three or four times a year, they had holidayed there, never tiring of the spectacular views. A small coastal area lucky enough to afford the scenery for free. A small caravan site set behind a housing estate; if you blinked then you could miss it. That was where they had always stayed, making regular holidaymakers there, true friends. A meeting up of liked minds.

Melinda had stayed there with her friend and neighbour since Peter's passing, as well as going there alone. Gone was the chance of them both ever doing it again together, more is the pity. She had so missed her husband's company and their holiday breaks. Life had changed so much in such a few short years. Treasure each day, she'd recalled people saying to her.

Now she knew how true that was. Life shouldn't be taken for granted, ever.

From the age of fifteen really, Peter had dominated her life. It may have taken two years before she had started courting him, so to speak, but he was there every weekend in the fish and chip shop presenting himself to her. It was only a matter of time before she had given in to his frequent proposals for a date.

The relationship had gone on from there and was still going strong forty-five years later, promptly ending with his death. Everything has to come to an end, Melinda had known; she'd not wanted it to. Peter was the strength in their relationship, there to provide love and comfort; keeping her from harm and supporting her throughout the years.

Spending a whole month in Fuerteventura after his passing, conversations with strangers there had evolved. One gentleman had, after hearing Melinda's story, suggested that Peter had taken her place in heaven. He would have struggled too, if honest, had Melinda died first but she had refused to think that way, even if that had been the case. Stephanie would have been there for her dad, Melinda knew.

Melinda's workplaces had all changed in Bristol. Gone was the insurance company she'd worked in before having Stephen. That was now a Mercure hotel, there for its visitors to enjoy the historical city of Bristol. Macfisheries had long gone, still a retail outlet but not of the food variations. Melinda hadn't ventured into Broadmead to find out exactly what merchandise was sold there now.

Norwich Union had closed down before being pulled down and demolished. Nothing structural wise stands there now. An empty space where a large company employing local people had been. Sad, but evidence of how times had changed, not always for the better. Greedy businesses wanting more, maybe; a certain trend altering today's times.

Even in South Wales, Melinda's working establishments had ceased to exist. The local public house where she had worked as a waitress after moving from Bristol, was now converted into a house. No longer used for anything of a commercial nature. The insurance jobs had closed permanently, one of them now a barber's shop; Melinda's dad's livelihood before retiring. The receptionist job, the building was burnt down in a fire and other jobs have seen the company move to newer premises further away. Her last working role, in the bookmaker's, is still going strong but has reduced the number of outlets open to the public. A gambling establishment that Melinda had been employed for eight years, only leaving due to ill health.

A sometimes cruel world of eventualities out of our control. Nothing today is permanent and cannot be taken for granted. Life is like a yo-yo, up and down all the time, unless you are very fortunate. Melinda wasn't one of the lucky ones. All said and done, Melinda's life had been lived and mostly devoured. She couldn't have complained about the parts of the globe she had travelled to and explored with Peter and the family over the years. Others around had fared a lot worse. She was spoilt there.

Their future plans together once retired, hadn't happened. Peter was too ill to manage anything written down on their bucket list. He had apologised to Melinda profusely, feeling so guilty about it. It was no one's fault. Fate had intervened and ruined their chance of any future beyond his early retirement, due to ill health and not by choice. That's how the cookie crumbles!

Melinda's life began in Totterdown, Bristol and will end somewhere, sometime. A mystery to Melinda. That day will be *A Moment in Time*.